LINE UPON LINE

ESSAYS ON MORMON DOCTRINE

LINE UPON LINE

ESSAYS ON MORMON DOCTRINE

Edited by

Gary James Bergera

Signature Books   Salt Lake City   1989

*For Leonard Arrington, Lester Bush, and Duane Jeffery —
who have made a difference*

Cover design: Easton Design

Interior design: Connie Disney

Library of Congress Cataloging-in-Publication Data

Line upon line : essays on Mormon doctrine / edited by Gary James
   Bergera.
      p.   cm.
   ISBN 0-941214-69-9
   1. Mormon Church—Doctrines.   2. Church of Jesus Christ of Latter-
Day Saints—Doctrines.   I. Bergera, Gary James.
BX8635.5.L56 1988
230'.93—dc19   88-30867
                                                                      CIP

COVER ILLUSTRATION: *THE TEMPLATE,* BY WOLF BARSCH, 1989, OIL ON CANVAS

CONTENTS

EDITOR'S INTRODUCTION

ONE OF THE DISTINGUISHING FEATURES OF THE CHURCH OF Jesus Christ of Latter-day Saints is a near absence of formal creeds or statements of binding doctrine. For all practical intents, the authoritative systematization of doctrine and theology does not exist, and deliberately so. As founding prophet Joseph Smith explained, "The most prominent difference in sentiment between the Latter-day Saints and sectarians [is] that the latter [are] all circumscribed by some peculiar creed, which deprive[s] its members of believing anything not contained therein, whereas the Latter-day Saints have no creed, but are ready to believe all true principles that exist, as they are made manifest from time to time."[1] This rejection of doctrinal creeds prompted one non-Mormon observer to label LDS beliefs as a kind of "do-it-yourself" theology.[2]

This is not to suggest, however, that the church possesses no mechanism for canonizing doctrine, by which it defines itself and its teachings in relation to other religions. For example, on 3 April 1976, during the church's semi-annual General Conference, Mormons from around the world participated in creating new canon by common consent. This canonizing process, however infrequently used, occupies a central, determining place in the formulation of official church doctrine (see also D&C 28:3; 26:2).

An important distinction exists between canon and other church-related discourse — "official" or otherwise. Despite statements equating all individual utterances inspired by the Holy Ghost (D&C 68:2-4) with binding institutional doctrine, inspired discourse and canon are not necessarily synonymous. If they were, it would have been unnecessary to present the Doctrine and Covenants to a general assembly of the church for its support in 1835, to present the Pearl of Great Price to a General Conference in 1880, to present church president Wilford Woodruff's Manifesto to members in 1890 for acceptance, or to present the official announcement regarding the eligibility of black Mormons to hold the priesthood to members in 1978 for their consent. In each instance, the sustaining vote of the general membership was required to change the status of the particular document from teaching or policy to official, institutional doctrine.

Needless to say, the canonization of some doctrines necessarily relegates others, however "true," to places of lesser institutional authority. That is, a teaching or doctrine may be true without being official or binding from an institutional perspective. Thus the writings of any Mormon—whether a General Authority, a regional leader, a local officer, or lay member anywhere—unless canonized, are secondary to the four printed "standard works" of the church— the Bible, the Book of Mormon, the Doctrine and Covenants, and the Pearl of Great Price—which contain the official, canonized doctrines of the church. "No revelation given through the head of the church ever becomes binding and authoritative upon members of the church," President Joseph F. Smith publicly explained, "until it has been presented to the church and accepted by them."[3] The process of canonization, Elder B. H. Roberts echoed, represents "the position of the Church . . . upon the authoritative sources of their doctrine."[4]

This distinction has at least two important applications for Mormons today. First, it affects the writings of church leaders and members who attempt to provide thorough, exhaustive, and especially "official" expositions of institutional doctrine and belief. Too often this kind of writing is used by otherwise well-meaning members to test and measure each another's orthodoxy. Such misuses are easily tempered by the fact that a healthy variety of competing—and occasionally conflicting— views and teachings exists. In the absence of authoritative, binding statements, no member's loyalty or commitment to the church should be questioned simply because his or her personal convictions differ from prevailing beliefs.

Second, the existence of a canonization process highlights the all-too-frequently ignored fact that the highest quorum in LDS church government is the general membership. This places the primary responsibility upon individual members for determining and evaluating canonized doctrine. Mormons must never retreat into the admittedly comfortable but ultimately irresponsible security of blind obedience from the trying, responsibility-laden path of reasoned and reasonable faith.

The genius of the LDS church regarding doctrine and theology is that it allows for, perhaps even requires, a diversity of views and opinions. As Hugh B. Brown, first counselor in the First Presidency, exhorted students at Brigham Young University in 1969, "We call upon you ... to exercise your God-given right to think through on every proposition that is submitted to you and be unafraid to express your opinions.... We are not so much concerned with whether your thoughts are orthodox or heterodox as we are that you shall have thoughts."[5] "If our members are ignorant of the doctrines," Apostle Boyd K. Packer later warned, "we are in danger, notwithstanding efficient programs and buildings."[6] A thoughtful, educated membership tends to be more stable than one that follows blindly.

Each of the sixteen essays selected for inclusion in *Line Upon Line* addresses a particular doctrinal or theological topic—usually one upon which different views and opinions exist. The authors—sensitive, cautious, and thoughtful—rely on a variety of authorities, approaches, and sources and make no pretense of trying to answer all questions or, more especially, of resolving what President J. Reuben Clark once described as "adventuresome expeditions" into "highly speculative principles and doctrines."[7] Instead, they hope to foster greater reflection and generate responsible discussion; to identify areas in need of more openness and tolerance; to note the relative strengths and weaknesses of various theological positions; and to suggest that differences of opinion, far from implying unorthodoxy, can indicate the presence of a genuine and sincere faith. Readers should know also that neither the authors nor the editor necessarily agrees with the views and conclusions reached in all of the essays that follow.

Appreciation is extended to the following publications for permission to reproduce, sometimes in a different format and/or under a different title, many of the essays appearing here: to *Dialogue: A Journal of Mormon Thought* for part or all of the essays by Boyd

Kirkland, Blake T. Ostler, George Boyd, and David John Buerger; and to *Sunstone* for essays by Thaddeus E. Shoemaker, Boyd Kirkland, Thomas G. Alexander, Van Hale, Kent E. Robson, Peter C. Appleby, Linda P. Wilcox, and Stephen L Richards. Three of the essays—"The Earliest Mormon Concept of God," by Dan Vogel; "The Development of the Concept of a Holy Ghost in Mormon Theology," by Vern Swanson; and "The Origin of the Human Spirit in Early Mormon Thought," by Van Hale—are published here for the first time.

— NOTES —

1. Joseph Smith, Jr., et al., *History of the Church of Jesus Christ of Latter-day Saints*, ed. B. H. Roberts, 2d ed. rev., 7 vols. (Salt Lake City: Deseret News, 1932-51), 5:215.

2. See Mark P. Leone, *Roots of Modern Mormonism* (Cambridge, MA: Harvard University Press, 1979), 7.

3. U.S. Senate, Committee on Privileges and Elections, *In the Matter of the Protests Against the Right of Hon. Reed Smoot, A Senator from the State of Utah to Hold His Seat*, 4 vols. (Washington, D.C.: Government Printing Office, 1906-1906), 1:96.

4. *Latter-day Saints' Millennial Star*, 83:516-19.

5. Hugh B. Brown, *Church News*, 24 May 1969.

6. Boyd K. Packer, "Principles," *Ensign*, March 1985, 9.

7. J. Reuben Clark, "When are the Writings or Sermons of Church Leaders Entitled to the Claim of Scripture?" *Church News*, 31 July 1954.

1.
Speculative Theology: Key to a Dynamic Faith

Thaddeus E. Shoemaker

SINCE THE ANCIENT GREEKS, THINKING PEOPLE HAVE LOOKED TO philosophy and theology to shed light on both the number and kind of problems with which the human family struggles. In the nineteenth century, Mormonism—followers and leaders alike—embraced a radical speculative theology. But many Mormons today seem to have abandoned this heritage of radical thought and have substituted hyperactivity for insightful inquiry. Put another way, they attempt to sustain their faith with works, believing that scriptural admonition and authority demand it. All too frequently church activity itself becomes an acceptable end to the expression of religion. Contemporary Mormons are generally content to live off the speculative insights of others, regardless of the contradictions inherent in such behavior.

This transformation resulted, I believe, from a lack of faith in the soundness of individual initiative, discussion, and decision regarding theological matters. Mormons appear in most instances to be content to be led and governed by the few in leadership positions. But even among the organizational heads there is a lack of speculative insight, if the quality of books and articles presently offered is evidence. Most Latter-day Saints are motivated by borrowed light rather than by insights and truths garnered by studious inquiry.

Ordinarily, this lack of inquiry describes the failure of any radical innovation to sustain itself for long. But Mormonism declares that every man is potentially a priest and every woman a priestess, each possessing unique powers embryonic in form and identical in substance to those possessed by deity. Mormon theology rejects the necessity of a hierarchy of spiritual elites and condemns such a notion as sectarian. Salvation, temporal and spiritual, is an individual responsibility. The church and its programs and activities are only processes to assist each member in working out his or her own salvation. No person can be saved in ignorance, but it is not the church's role to dispel ignorance. Rather it is the individual's responsibility to seek knowledge and then use the church and its resources to help apply this new insight. To place the church and its leadership in the role of saviors is sacrilegious and denies that most sacred of all doctrines and principles, free agency. Each Latter-day Saint will be held accountable for the amount of knowledge he or she possesses, and on this will all ultimately be judged.

Why do so many of the Saints seem to resist such self-scrutiny? It is an error to assume that raising questions (or speculating) about the restored gospel leads to apostasy. If the gospel of Jesus Christ embraces all truth regardless of where it is found, then seekers will welcome the challenges and tests that come from the free exchange of ideas and beliefs. Revealed truth requires individual initiative, discussion, and decision regarding all of life's questions. This is particularly true with regard to theological ones.

Speculative theology serves the same purpose for the gospel of Jesus Christ as does the philosophy of religion for the field of philosophy. Speculative theology is not necessarily concerned with justifying or disparaging any particular belief, doctrine, or practice of Mormonism, nor is it concerned solely with the plausibility or reasonableness of the church's dogma and teachings. Speculative theology tests the church's claim of possessing special and vitally important knowledge about the nature of the world and universe and the role of men and women in them. Properly pursued, it leads not to agnosticism or atheism. Neither does one have to be agnostic or atheist to engage in this intellectual endeavor. No, properly pursued, speculation leads to an affirmation — a continuing renewal, not destruction, although a destructive element is present — of one's faith. In other words, speculative theology affirms the very things it questions.

The crucial issue for speculative theology is recognizing that in revealing truth God seldom explains why he commands or instructs. Finding out why becomes an individual search. Our desire to know causes unexpected consternations and at times agonies. We accept what God has said on faith — the essential initial step if the journey to eternal life is ever to begin. However, progression is minimal if faith does not lead to knowledge.

Speculative theology recognizes that knowledge of the truth is always partially destructive to faith. Scriptural instruction is precise on this matter (see Al. 32:17–27). But it is wrong to assume that the pursuit of knowledge through speculation should be avoided because of its destructive qualities. Learning and growth include and proceed from the "destructive" process called "positive disintegration." All knowledge destroys the faith it replaces, calling into existence the need for newer and more dynamic faith. Because we are both imperfect in our apprehension of knowledge and are unable to perfectly apply it to reality, new questions are raised for which answers are sought. The cycle is repeated and the continuous application of this process Mormonism calls eternal progression.

Speculative theology avoids the negativism which sometimes accompanies intellectual inquiry, because creative doubt proceeds from the converse of skepticism — doubts arise because sufficient knowledge is lacking. Creative doubt leads to growth and fulfillment because it motivates a desire to know the consequences of continued questioning, inquiring, and applying what we know to real life. Concomitantly, and in some way inextricably, is the concept of incrementalism — that knowledge is acquired (and lost) step by step. However, the key to its retention is found in how, in what way, and for what reason it is applied in our lives. Activity multiplied by activity, unquestioningly doing "one's duty" without understanding, will not reward or fulfill, nor will it sustain faith. For personal growth and development are as important as the efficient functioning of the church. The institution is a means to exaltation, never the end. Thus the church is truly a hospital for sinners, not a museum for the Saints. If there were no sin one would not need the church — even the perfect "true" one — just as one would not need a hospital — even a perfect one — if there were no illness or disease.

Related to positive disintegration, creative doubt, and incrementalism are the epistemological forms, structures, and methods of speculative theology. The diverse elements of Mormonism's epistemology (its theory of knowledge), lacking synthesis, are scattered throughout its doctrine and practices and are meaningful only as they are circumscribed by free agency. The concepts embraced by speculative theology as I see them are reason, experience, authority, intuition, and imagination. In one way or another these structures and methods are products of the mind and conscience.

Reason. Briefly, reason is the mental and/or intellectual processes by which data, facts, information, etc., are organized into a systematic order to provide understanding and meaning. Reason's method is logic; its faculty, the mind; and its process, thinking. This capacity for rational discrimination and decision-making sets humans apart from others of God's creatures.

The human faculty of the mind, with its facility to reason, makes free agency meaningful. Through choices humans become moral agents and accountable for their actions. Rational faculties permit us to learn vicariously, and thus we expand our universe considerably beyond our experiential world.

The mind, continually expanding, growing, and developing, is the seat of knowledge. Its station and relationship to the rest of our faculties are demonstrated in these instructions to Joseph Smith's friend and scribe Oliver Cowdery: "But behold, I say unto you, that you must study it out in your *mind*; then you must ask me if it be right, and if it is right I will cause that your bosom shall burn within you; therefore you shall *feel* that it is right" (D&C 9, emphasis added).

Beyond this, the mind is the repository of will. The mind is intended to be the power by which emotions and subconscious drives are regulated and kept within the bounds of propriety. Self-control and self-will are properly referred to as mental activities.

Experience. According to Mormon teachings, as intelligences we were all organized spiritually prior to being born physically into mortality. God in organizing or creating us provided the spiritual bodies in which the intelligences reside. As spirit beings under the direction of God, literally our father through spiritual creation, we grew, developed, and fulfilled ourselves until the time appointed for our entrance into mortality. Through our physical creation, our bodies became the tabernacles for our spirits, and we entered mortality by the process we call birth.

Experience is usually defined as the conjunction of perception (physical senses) and reality. Its method is empirical; its faculty, the sense and the mind; and its process, observation. In a more formal and structured way, experience translates to experimentation. Out of experimentations and experiences come discoveries of eternal importance. Reason does not destroy faith; it perfects it and makes the physical laws our servants, not our masters. Reason makes possible the command to "subdue the earth" (Gen. 1:28).

Authority. Members of the Church of Jesus Christ of Latter-day Saints have authorities in abundance. I do not mean to suggest that we have too many, but there is always a danger of factionalism and favoritism in having so many. This danger is magnified because of the proclivity of many Mormons to rely on church activity and on the insights of others to assuage their doubts.

There is one sense in Mormonism in which authority has a precise meaning. It deals with the delegation of priesthood power from God to men and women and the ecclesiastical function of authority in church order and liturgy. However, in the epistemological definition of authority, Mormonism is fraught with ambiguity and confusion. Speculative theology plays an insightful and meaningful role in helping the individual find his or her way in the maze of competing and conflicting authorities on critical theological issues and questions.

Intuition. Intuition, revelation, and inspiration are unique learning forms, and just as the condition of the mind helps to determine the knowledge gained from experience, so the condition of the conscience helps to determine the knowledge received through intuition. The method of intuition is inspiration and revelation, its faculty is the conscience, and its process is prayer, meditation, and prophecy. By definition, intuition is comprehension and understanding by non-intellectual perception and means. By and large such learning resists empirical verification of the usual sort. The major device by which intuition becomes functional is the conscience, and it appears that the conscience is responsive to both spiritual and physical stimuli. But the conscience also seems to serve as a kind of built-in regulator that provides stability and inter-harmony. If we ignore the warning signals of our conscience, we place our personalities in jeopardy.

Imagination. The human personality possesses a great variety of feelings and sensitivities. Emotions and imaginations have inspired some of the greatest human efforts in art, literature, philosophy, theology, and music. They have also produced great tragedy and human suffering. But this is not sufficient reason to malign fantasy and daydreaming. Positive daydreaming and creative imagining are essential parts of the human personality and should inspire us to make the world a more beautiful and rewarding place to live. These most basic of human qualities will make us "God-like" and "Christ-like." They brighten, uplift, and inspire creative productivity and awaken the restorative powers of the worth of self and others.

Speculative theology is essential, its substance and form crucial to a progressive lifestyle. It inspires by the questions it raises; it fulfills and rewards by the answers it produces; it makes for a creative and exciting existence; and its consequences reach into the eternities. Speculative theology produces a more dynamic faith and awakens deep within the soul a primal longing for that eternal reunion with Father and Mother whereby we may know all that they know, do all that they do, and be all that they are.

2.
Defining the Contemporary Mormon Concept of God

Van Hale

FOR CENTURIES, BELIEVING CHRISTIANS HAVE TRIED TO CODIFY, clarify, and classify their many different doctrines of God. They have asked: Who is God? Who is the Son? Who is the Holy Ghost? Who is Jesus? Who is the Word? Who is the Father? How are they one? and How are they distinct?

The variety of answers to these and other questions has sometimes led to controversies of a life-or-death nature. In Mormon history disagreement over such doctrines was a major cause of dissension between Joseph Smith and one of his counselors in the First Presidency, William Law. Even today, a major difference between the LDS church and its fundamentalist offshoots concerns the doctrine of deity.

Because an individual's concept of deity can affect his or her spiritual (and in many instances temporal) standing, it may be helpful to become familiar with the terms, classes, and categories used in discussing this topic. While analyzing a list of terms may not seem important — after all, it is understanding the doctrine of deity which is important, not so much the language used to express it — comparing and contrasting such theological ideas can result in a better understanding of many of the teachings about the nature of God.

Other Christians use a variety of terms to describe their concept of the Almighty, but there is no commonly recognized term to define the Mormon doctrine of deity. There are three ways we might wish to solve this problem: borrow an appropriate term;

combine or modify existing terms; or create new terms. The use of Christian terms is probably most useful, since it allows us to communicate more readily with the wider Christian community.

Of course, there are some problems in attempting to apply these terms to Mormonism. First, because of the complexity of ideas and the ambiguity of terms, it is seldom easy to define precisely any doctrine of deity. Second, doctrines of deity are often broadened, deepened, or in some way changed through continued pondering and debating and also through the passing of time. Thus, perfect consistency is not to be expected.

This tendency toward development is particularly apparent in Mormonism, because it denies that God's revelation of himself reached its fullness at the beginning of the Christian era. Mormonism does not look back to a completed revelation; it seeks further insight through continuing revelation. There is no better example of this than Joseph Smith's own doctrine of God, which clearly passed through stages of development—development which he himself acknowledged (see, for example, D&C 50:40; 42:61; 88:49; 121:28). In fact, Smith once indicated that it was not until he was working on the Book of Abraham (no earlier than 1835) that he had learned "that God, the Father of Jesus Christ, had a father . . . and that He had a Father also."[1] This concept of continuing revelation makes the defining of doctrine precarious and demonstrates the need for several terms to define Mormon doctrine at its various stages of development.

The terms describing different theological positions might best be organized into three groups of questions: (1) In Mormon doctrine how many gods are there? Specifically, is Mormon doctrine monotheistic, polytheistic, tritheistic, or henotheistic? (2) What is the Mormon concept of the Godhead? Unitarian, binitarian, or trinitarian? (3) And what is the Mormon doctrine of the oneness of the Godhead? Monarchian, modalistic, homoousion, or homoiousion?

Etymologically, monotheism means "one god." But the term "one god" is subject to interpretation. One attempt to define Mormonism as monotheistic is that of Mormon General Authority Bruce R. McConkie, who states in *Mormon Doctrine* that monotheism, when properly interpreted, means "that the Father, Son, and Holy Ghost— each of whom is a separate and distinct godly personage—are one

God, meaning one Godhead."[2] This, however, redefines mono-theism and does not account for the fact that Mormonism teaches the existence of gods who are not the Father, Son, or Holy Ghost. Such a redefinition tends to confuse or mislead those who under-stand the term to refer more commonly to the belief in one supreme personal being without superiors, equals, or others of the same na-ture. The value of a term can be greatly diminished if it must be redefined.

Another way to define Mormonism as monotheistic was that of Apostle Orson Pratt and B. H. Roberts, of the Seventy, who be-lieved in an impersonal power or attribute, the "Divine Nature," which is shared by all who are gods. Roberts called this the "God of all other Gods." This approach suggests that the "Divine Nature" is the one true God, thus making Mormonism monotheistic.[3] However, such a theory has not been popular among Mormons and was even denounced by Brigham Young and other church authorities in 1860.[4] In addition, it represents another misapplication of the term "monotheism."

Some Mormon writers have argued that in its early stages Mormonism was monotheistic. For example, early Mormon scrip-tures—the Book of Mormon and the Doctrine and Covenants—not only declare Father, Son, and Holy Ghost to be one God (D&C 20:27, 28; Al. 11:44) but state that Jesus and the Father are identical—that is, that Jesus was the Father come in the flesh (Mos. 7:27; 15:1–5; Eth. 4:12). In addition, several statements in early Mormon scriptures explicitly deny the existence of more than one God. For instance, in the Book of Alma, Amulek tells Zeezrom that there is one God only and explains that the Son of God is the very Eternal Father (Al. 11:26–39; cf. D&C 20:17–19; Moses 1:6).

At the same time, other passages do not appear to support simple monotheism. For example, throughout 3 Nephi a clear dis-tinction is made between the Father who is in heaven and the Son who is on earth (3 Ne. 11:6–8, 32; 15:1, 18, 19; 18:27; 26:2, 5, 15). In addition, any argument on this point must consider Joseph Smith's own interpretation of his early teachings. In 1844 he said, "I have always declared God to be a distinct personage, Jesus Christ a sepa-rate and distinct personage from God the Father, and that the Holy Ghost was a distinct personage and a spirit."[5] Thus, that Mormonism initially was monotheistic can only be said with reservation, and it would certainly be inaccurate to define Mormon doctrine since the 1840s as monotheistic.

Generally, Mormons have been unwilling to adopt the term "polytheism." But since polytheism refers to a belief in the existence of more than one god—clearly a Mormon doctrine—why have Latter-day Saints refused to use this common term to define their doctrine of God? The answer is that while the term is appropriate, the technical definition is not the only consideration in this instance. Through the centuries, polytheism has been used to refer to ancient systems of gods totally foreign, if not repugnant, to contemporary Mormonism. As a result, tradition has imbued it with a negative connotation. Today, only Mormonism's opponents apply the term "polytheism" to LDS beliefs. A more acceptable term to Mormons is "plurality of gods." This phrase conveys the doctrine of many gods without polytheism's negative connotations.

Literally, tritheism means three gods. The term was coined in the sixth century by opponents of John Philopon to refer to what they considered to be a heretical doctrine of the Godhead. "According to him, there are many men each with his own essence but 'through their common form all men are one,' so that in this sense they all have the same essence. In similar fashion he conceived the relation of the three persons of the Trinity."[6] Because Philopon saw the Father, Son, and Holy Ghost as having distinct natures, his detractors claimed that he believed in three Gods, although it is unclear if he would have actually confessed such a belief.

Joseph Smith, on the other hand, did believe that the Father, Son, and Holy Ghost "constitute[d] three distinct personages and three Gods."[7] Thus tritheism may be a valuable term for discussing Mormon doctrine. It is simple and transparent, and although created by opponents of the idea, it does not have polytheism's negative connotation. However, it does refer only to three gods in the Godhead without acknowledging the existence of other gods.

Henotheism is the worship of one God while acknowledging, or at least not denying, the existence of other gods. At first glance, this term seems to apply to contemporary Mormonism, especially in light of this statement from Joseph Smith's last public discourse: "I say there are Gods many and Lords many, but to us only one, and we are to be in subjection to that one."[8] However, it is important to understand that the term was invented by a nineteenth-century German scholar, Max Mueller, to refer to what he and others believed was the faith of early Israel and denotes the worship of a god who is confined to a specific geographical area. For example, some scholars believe that originally Jehovah was the god of Sinai whose jurisdiction did not extend to Canaan, which was another god's territory. Thus while the basic concept is similar to Mormonism, henotheism would probably not accurately communicate Mormon beliefs to those familiar with the technical use of the term.

The terms "unitarian," "binitarian," and "trinitarian" have all been used to describe the Godhead. Unitarianism, which holds that there is but one member of the Godhead, is committed to the idea of oneness — one God, one person, one nature. This concept was proclaimed by a sizeable number of early Christians prior to the formulation of the trinitarian creeds of the fourth and fifth centuries. However, the term "unitarian" was coined in 1600 to identify a strong anti-trinitarian movement which started in Europe and was transplanted to America in the eighteenth century. In the United States, the unitarian controversy peaked between 1815 and 1833 in New England, where Joseph Smith spent his early years.

Some writers have suggested that Mormon doctrine was initially unitarian. However, this assertion seems unlikely. One of the central theological issues of the 1820s was the deity of Jesus Christ. The Unitarians denied that Jesus was God.[9] Yet this teaching is precisely the opposite of that taught in the Book of Mormon, which, beginning with the title page, repeatedly declares the deity of Jesus Christ. Mormonism certainly does not accept unitarian doctrine today, nor does it appear ever to have done so.

The term "binitarian" was coined in 1890 to refer to some early Christian theologians who believed in two persons in the Godhead. While the term does not describe Mormon doctrine since the 1840s, there is one important doctrinal statement which seems to have a binitarian emphasis. The "Lectures on Faith," which appeared in all editions of the Doctrine and Covenants from 1835 to 1921, states that "there are two personages who constitute the great, matchless, governing and supreme power over all things. . . . They are the Father and the Son." Elsewhere it instructs, "How many personages are there in the Godhead? Two: the Father and the Son." The lecture goes on to teach that these two personages possess the same mind, "which mind is the Holy Spirit . . . and these constitute the Godhead, and are one." This lecture does not present the Holy Ghost as a spirit being, a doctrine taught a few years later. I believe there is value in using the term "binitarian" in reference to the doctrine of this period.

The first person to use the term "trinity" was apparently early Latin church father Tertullian at the beginning of the third century. Since that time it has been used loosely to refer to virtually any idea which mentions three and one in reference to the Godhead. However, around the fifth or sixth century, the term acquired a precise definition, which provides the basis for meaningful use of the term and which is perhaps best expressed in the Athanasian Creed: three distinct persons of one undivided substance.

Throughout history many Christians have departed from the strict doctrine of this creed, emphasizing either the oneness or the threeness. Some have declared the Father, Son, and Holy Ghost to be only one divine person; others have declared that the divine substance is divided into Father, Son, and Holy Ghost, and have been charged with tritheism. However, these extremes cannot tech- nically be called trinitarianism.

Has Mormon doctrine ever been trinitarian? A number of Mormon writers have used the word "trinity" to define the Mormon doctrine of the Godhead, including apostles James E. Talmage[10] and Richard L. Evans.[11] Nevertheless, such usage redefines the term. The technical denotation does not apply to contemporary Mormonism.

Some have claimed that the Book of Mormon and other early revelations suggest that Mormon doctrine began as trinitarian. However, this also must be rejected since these same early Mormon writings so emphasize the oneness of the Father and the Son as to declare "that the Son is the Father, and the Father is the Son" (Joseph Smith Translation, Luke 10:23; cf. Mos. 15; 16:15; Al. 11:38, 39; Eth. 4:12; 3:14).

Finally, what of the Mormon doctrine of the oneness of the Godhead? Is it monarchian, modalistic, homoousion, or homo- iousion?

Monarchianism was coined by Tertullian to denote a doc- trine which flourished in the third century. It resulted from some Christians who wanted to avoid any possible charge of polytheism by proclaiming the oneness of God and by accounting for Jesus and the Holy Ghost in a manner which could not in any way be thought to compromise that oneness. In other words, it was strict mono-theism.

This doctrine appears in two forms. The first is dynamic monarchianism. "Dynamic" means "power" and refers to the doc-trine that the power of the one God rested upon Jesus, who was not himself a god. Since Mormonism has always taught that Jesus was God before coming in the flesh (see Mos. 3:5; 4:2; 7:27; 1 Ne. 11:16), there appears to be no value in applying this term to any doctrine in LDS history.

The second form is modalism, which teaches that the Father, Son, and Holy Ghost are not three persons or distinctions but rather three modes of divine expression of the one God. This doctrine proclaims both the oneness of God and the deity of Jesus. While this concept is foreign to current Mormon doctrine, there are similari-ties between the teachings of several early modalists and some state-ments in the Book of Mormon. For example, Tertullian records one modalist teaching at the beginning of the third century that "the Father Himself came down into the Virgin, and was Himself born of her, Himself suffered, indeed was Himself Jesus Christ."[12] The con-cept that Jesus Christ was the Father, took upon himself flesh by birth, and suffered for humanity seems to be taught in several Book of Mormon passages (Mos. 7:27; 13:34; 15:1-5; 16:15; Eth. 3:14; 4:7-12).

But before concluding that modalism is the term to define Mormon doctrine, it must be recognized that the Book of Mormon contains several other passages which seem to contradict the one-ness of modalism (e.g., 3 Ne. 11:6-8, 32; 15:1, 18, 19; 18:27; 26:2, 5, 15). Thus, while there may be value in using modalism to discuss Book of Mormon doctrine, one would be well advised to avoid using the term comprehensively.

Two other terms worth examining are "homoousion" and "homoiousion"—Greek words which figured prominently in the theological controversies of the fourth century. "Homoousios" was the term used in the Nicene Creed to identify the substance of the Son as the substance of the Father. That is, the Son was considered by some as homoousios (of the same substance) with the Father. The term "homoiousios," on the other hand, was used by some oppo-nents of the Nicene Creed to declare that the Son was not of the same substance but rather of like substance with the Father.

Homoiousios might well be used to define Mormon doctrine, which does declare the Father and the Son to be of like substance but not of the same substance.

By now it should be clear that even though Mormon doctrine can be compared and contrasted to a dozen Christian terms, a precise theological term for the Mormon doctrine of deity is still not readily available. One solution might be to create an entirely new category, such as B. H. Roberts's phrase, "the Mormon doctrine of deity." But this is too vague. Another solution might be to combine historic theological terms to define the Mormon doctrine of deity as a development from a homoousion, modalistic monarchian form of monotheism to homoiousion, tritheistic henotheism. But this much technical jargon is too cumbersome for anyone to take seriously.

Perhaps there is some solace in our as-yet unfruitful quest for precise definition. For should we ever succeed in producing the terminology to define the contemporary Mormon doctrine of deity, we might also succumb to the long-resisted temptation to produce a rigid Mormon creed, stifling the open-ended nature of revelation and suppressing the possibility of acquiring new insights in the future.

– NOTES –

1. Joseph Smith et al., *History of the Church of Jesus Christ of Latter-day Saints*, ed. B. H. Roberts, 2nd ed. rev., 7 vols. (Salt Lake City: Deseret News, 1932–51), 6:476 (hereafter HC, followed by volume and page numbers).

2. Bruce R. McConkie, *Mormon Doctrine*, 2nd ed. (Salt Lake City: Bookcraft, 1966), 463.

3. See Truman G. Madsen, "The Meaning of Christ—The Truth, The Way, The Life: An Analysis of B. H. Roberts's Unpublished Masterwork," *Brigham Young University Studies* 15 (Spring 1975), 3:289; Gary James Bergera, "The Orson Pratt-Brigham Young Controversies: Conflict Within the Quorums, 1853 to 1868," *Dialogue: A Journal of Mormon Thought* 13 (Summer 1980), 2:11.

4. Bergera, 17–20, 33–35.

5. HC 6:474.

6. In *The New Schaff-Herzog Encyclopedia of Religion and Ethics*, 12:24.

7. HC 6:474.

8. Ibid.

9. See Bruce M. Stephens, *God's Last Metaphor: The Doctrine of the Trinity in New England Theology* (1981).

10. See James E. Talmage, *The Articles of Faith* (Salt Lake City, 1890).

11. See Richard L. Evans, in Leo Rosten, *Religions in America* (1952).

12. *The Ante-Nicene Fathers,* 3:597.

3.
The Earliest Mormon Concept of God

Dan Vogel

THE FOUNDING DOCUMENT OF JOSEPH SMITH'S CHURCH OF Christ—its "Articles and Covenants"—declared in June 1830 that the "Father, Son, and Holy Ghost is one God, infinite and eternal, without end."[1] Because of ambiguity in this early "Mormon Creed" many outsiders concluded that the Mormon view of God was similar to orthodox trinitarian creeds.[2] A growing number of scholars today, recognizing that the Mormon concept of God changed as revelations expanded and clarified previous beliefs, have suggested that the earliest Mormon doctrine, at least before 1835, was "essentially trinitarian."[3] In contrast, I believe that Mormonism was never trinitarian but consistently preferred heterodox definitions of God.

For the earliest Mormon view, one must turn first to the Book of Mormon. According to Reformed Baptist preacher and early Mormon critic Alexander Campbell, one of the "great controversies" which the Book of Mormon tried to decide was the nature of "the trinity."[4] Although Campbell did not discuss in detail the Book of Mormon's position on the subject, he was aware of the various contemporary debates over the nature of the Godhead.

Campbell and his contemporaries struggled over the same problems about the Christian God which had plagued Christendom for centuries. Discussion especially centered on the relationship between the Father and the Son. Were the Father and Son the same being? Or two distinct persons? Were both gods? If so, in what sense could it be said that there is only one god? If the Father alone was

God, what was the status of the Son? The nature of God was a serious issue in early nineteenth-century America and sharply divided various religious groups.

The three major denominations in the United States—Presbyterian, Methodist, and Baptist—were "orthodox" trinitarians, a doctrine they inherited from Catholicism. As trinitarians they held that the Father, Son, and Holy Ghost represented three "persons" but one divine "substance." This was a non-rational way of explaining the threeness of the Godhead without abandoning monotheism—the belief in one God only. The Father is God, the Son is God, and the Holy Ghost is God; yet in some mystical manner there is only one God. The concept may have been understood by theologians, but its subtleties escaped the layperson and preacher, who sometimes gave definitions of God considered heretical by their own superiors.

Perhaps the most radical solution to the problem of God's nature was put forward by the Unitarians and Universalists, who maintained that the Father only was God. In his *Treatise on Atonement*, Hosea Ballou rejected the orthodox belief in the deity of Jesus and objected to the idea that "God himself, assumed a body of flesh and blood . . . and suffered the penalty of the law by death, and arose from the dead."[5] Thus Ballou and other Unitarians not only denied Jesus' divinity but discarded the idea of a vicarious atonement.

Others, especially those who attempted to "restore" Christianity to its primitive condition—including Alexander Campbell, Baptist Abner Jones of Vermont, and Presbyterian Barton W. Stone of Kentucky—sought solutions somewhere between the orthodoxy of trinitarianism and the radicalism of Unitarianism.[6] Primitivists in nineteenth-century America avoided the term "Trinity" when describing the Godhead. Not only was the word not found in the Bible (the term had been introduced by Theophilus, Bishop of Antioch, in the second century), but it carried the connotation of Catholic creedalism. Most in the primitive gospel movement were not trinitarians. Barton W. Stone, for example, confessed that during his early days as a Presbyterian he had "stumbled at the doctrine of the Trinity as taught in the Confession."[7]

David Millard, a binitarian, said of Primitivists in the "Christian Connexion," "with very few exceptions, they are not Trinitarians, averring that they can neither find the word nor the doctrine in the Bible." Instead, "they believe 'the Lord our Jehovah is *one* Lord,' and purely *one*. That 'Jesus Christ is the only begotten Son of God.' That the Holy Ghost is that divine unction with which our Saviour was anointed, (Acts x. 38,) the effusion that was poured out on the day of Pentecost; and that it is a divine emanation of God, by which he exerts an energy or influence on rational minds. While they believe that Jesus Christ is the Son of God, they are not Socinians or Humanitarians. Their prevailing belief is that Jesus Christ existed with the Father before all worlds."[8] In other words, at least some Primitivists, including Millard, were binitarian, believing that the Godhead consisted of two persons but denying the person of the Holy Ghost, which was "a divine emanation of God."

Primitivists were not bitheists (literally a belief in two distinct gods). Nor did they believe Jesus was merely human as did Socinians, Humanitarians, and Unitarians. Millard held the Primitivist belief that the Son was divine in the sense that his Father was God. Human fathers have sons who are separate beings from themselves but have the same human nature. In the same way, the Son of God is a separate being from the Father but with the same divine nature and therefore may be called the Father's "proper son."[9] Some have associated this view of God with Unitarianism, but Primitivists in the Christian Connection would have seen their position as distinct.[10] More precisely, the Primitivists' view of God was closest to "dynamic" monarchianism: Jesus was divine only in the sense that he shared God's power, but he was not a god himself.[11]

As a Primitivist, Alexander Campbell also objected to the "Calvinistic doctrine of the Trinity," as well as to the use of the term "Trinity."[12] But although he attacked the "unintelligible jargon, the unmeaning language of the orthodox creeds on this subject" of the Trinity, he nevertheless held that the Father, Son, and Holy Spirit were "three Divine persons in one Divine nature."[13] Despite this trinitarian-sounding statement, some of Campbell's contemporaries accused him of having a bitheistic view of God.[14] And one scholar of Campbell's theology concluded that Campbell held a position "consistent with binitarian ideas."[15]

The heterodox view of God which theologians refer to as modalism (or Sabellianism) was also included in the theological discussion preoccupying early nineteenth-century America. Sabellius was a third-century heretic who held that "the Son Himself is the Father, and *vise versa*."[16] Modalists conceived the Father, Son, and Holy Ghost as three modes or expressions of the one God. A favorite illustration is taken from the sun: just as the sun is round and bright and hot but is actually one sun, not three realities, so we perceive a certain threeness in God, although in actuality he is one being.[17] Modalism thus differs from orthodox definitions of the Godhead in that it does not distinguish between the "person" of the Father and the "person" of the Son. In other words, the Father not only begets the Son but becomes the Son; Jesus is literally both Son and Father. This position is also sometimes called "patripassianism," because the Father in the person of the Son suffers on the cross.

David Millard, who spent a great deal of time combatting trinitarianism in western New York, described in 1818 "some Trinitarians" who "reject the term *person*, and instead of this, use the term *mode*, or *office*: and hold that the Trinity consists in one God, acting in three distinct *offices*."[18] In 1823 Millard's well-known book, *The True Messiah*, was published in Canandaigua, New York. This 214-page treatise on the Godhead not only presents Millard's binitarian views but also contains his reasons for rejecting trinitarianism, including "Sabellianism." After describing the position of the ancient Sabellians, Millard noted: "A great part of Trinitarians are now on the same ground, viz. that one God only acts in three distinct offices. They sometimes indeed call those offices *persons*, as they say for want of a better *term*, but when confuted upon the ground of *three persons*, they immediately assert that God acts in three *offices*, which is direct Sabellianism. It is therefore worthy of remark, how near many Trinitarians approach to the old doctrine of *Sabellianism*."[19]

The Book of Mormon appeared in March 1830 against this backdrop of theological debate. The book's express purpose was to correct false doctrine current in nineteenth-century America (2 Ne. 3:12). It is therefore impossible to understand the earliest Mormon concept of God without reconstructing the social and theological context in which Mormonism emerged. How does the Book of Mormon's theology compare with the various views of God being debated at the time of its publication? How did the Book of Mormon's first readers interpret its position on the subject? How was the Book of Mormon's theology viewed by its opponents? Was its theology orthodox, heterodox, or unique?

Those in the early nineteenth century who took the time to closely examine the Book of Mormon recognized that its theology was far from orthodox. Joseph Smith's mother, Lucy, recalled that shortly after the Book of Mormon was published the Methodists "rage[d]" at its concept of God because it conflicted with their creed.[20] As late as 1837, one outsider commented on the Book of Mormon's unorthodox view of God.[21] There were legitimate reasons for the first readers of the Book of Mormon to conclude that its theology conflicted with orthodox creeds.

Modern students of the Book of Mormon have reached the same conclusion, even if they differ on what exactly the Book of Mormon proposes. Perhaps the least likely comparison has been between Book of Mormon theology and Unitarianism[22] — least likely, because the Book of Mormon is Christ-centered and repeatedly affirms the deity of Jesus (title page; 1 Ne. 11:13-21; Mos. 15:1; Eth. 2:12) and the doctrine of vicarious atonement (Mos. 3:11, 15-16). No one has so far considered a comparison to the binitarianism or "dynamic" monarchianism of the Christian Connection. These Primitivists, unlike Unitarians, would have agreed with the Book of Mormon's position on Jesus' atonement but rejected its outspoken assertion that Jesus is God.

As suggested, most modern scholars have concluded that both the Book of Mormon and the early Mormon concept of God was closest to trinitarianism. Those who see trinitarianism in the Book of Mormon usually refer to 3 Nephi, where the resurrected Jesus declares to the Nephites: "I bear record of the Father, and the Father beareth record of me, and the Holy Ghost beareth record of the Father and me . . . for the Father, and I, and the Holy Ghost are one" (11:32, 36; compare 1 Jn. 5:7).[23] However, *all* theological positions on the Godhead include the concept of oneness. Trinitarians and modalists interpret unity passages literally, while binitarians, bitheists, and Unitarians interpret them allegorically. Thus the important question becomes in what sense the Book of Mormon speaks of the oneness of the Godhead. That the Book of Mormon includes passages about the oneness of God does not necessarily establish it as trinitarian.[24]

A major difficulty in defining the Book of Mormon as trinitarian is its failure to clearly distinguish between the person of the Father and the person of the Son. This is especially apparent when the book declares that Jesus is both Father and Son. Passages which speak of the Father sending the Son (Al. 14:5; 3 Ne. 27:13–14; 26:5) do not necessarily support a trinitarian view and should be understood in light of Ether 4:12: "He that will not believe me will not believe the Father who sent me. For behold, I am the Father." In other words, Jesus as the Father sent himself into the world to redeem his people. Nor do passages which speak of the Son being prepared from before the foundation of the earth (Mos. 18:13) necessarily imply two persons existing before the incarnation. Consider the following: "I am he who was prepared from the foundation of the world to redeem my people. Behold, I am Jesus Christ. I am the Father and the Son" (Eth. 3:14). The Book of Mormon therefore violates a major tenet of trinitarianism by confusing the persons of the Father and Son and by referring to Jesus as the Father.

However, such ambiguities do suggest that the view of God which comes closest to that of the Book of Mormon is modalism or Sabellianism.[25] Modalistic elements such as the literal oneness of the Godhead, the Father becoming the Son, and patripassianism are clearly expressed in the Book of Mormon.

The Book of Mormon's description of the incarnation is congruent with the patripassianism of modalism. King Benjamin, for example, tells his people that "the time cometh, and is not far distant, that with power, the Lord Omnipotent who reigneth, who was, and is from all eternity to all eternity, shall come down from heaven among the children of men, and shall dwell in a tabernacle of clay. . . . And he shall be called Jesus Christ, the Son of God, the Father of heaven and earth, the Creator of all things from the beginning" (Mos. 3:5, 8).

Other passages make it clear that Jesus is literally the Father. As a pre-mortal spirit being, Jesus appeared to the brother of Jared and declared: "I am the Father and the Son" (Eth. 3:14) and "He that will not believe me will not believe the Father who sent me. For behold, I am the Father" (4:12). Jesus further explained, "This body, which ye now behold, is the body of my spirit; and man have I created after the body of my spirit; and even as I appear unto thee to be in the spirit will I appear unto my people in the flesh" (3:16).

Similarly, Nephi's experience near the time of Jesus' birth suggested the same identity between Jesus and the Father. Samuel the Lamanite had predicted the signs which would precede Jesus' birth, that his people "might know of the coming of Jesus Christ, the Son of God, the Father of heaven and of earth, the Creator of all things from the beginning" (He. 14:12). On the day previous to Jesus' birth, the "voice of the Lord" came to Nephi: "I come . . . to do the will, both of the Father and of the Son — of the Father because of *me*, and of the Son because of *my* flesh" (3 Ne. 1:14, my emphasis).

The first part of the Book of Mormon describes the "condescension of God" (1 Ne. 11:16, 26). But the first edition of the book gives a much more literal reading of the incarnation than do later editions. Nephi, for example, is told that the "virgin" which he saw in vision was "the mother of God, after the manner of the flesh."[26] When Nephi sees the virgin "bearing a child in her arms," the angel declares, "Behold the Lamb of God, yea, even the Eternal Father."[27]

The Book of Mormon expresses the literal oneness demanded by modalism. Zeerom, for example, asked Amulek two important questions on the nature of the Godhead. First: "Is there more than one God?", to which Amulek answered, "No." Second: "Is the Son of God the very Eternal Father?", to which Amulek answered, "Yea, he is the very Eternal Father of heaven and of earth . . . and he shall come into the world to redeem his people" (Al. 11:28–29, 38–39). Thus the Book of Mormon was written to prove that "JESUS is the CHRIST, the ETERNAL GOD" (title page).

Book of Mormon prophet Abinadi also explained the oneness of the Father and the Son in words that modalists would easily understand: "God himself shall come down among the children of men, and shall redeem his people. And because he dwelleth in flesh he shall be called the Son of God, and having subjected the flesh to the will of the Father, being the Father and the Son — the Father, because he was conceived by the power of God; and the Son, because of the flesh; thus becoming the Father and Son — and they are one God, yea, the very Eternal Father of heaven and of earth. And thus the flesh becoming subject to the Spirit, or the Son to the Father, being one God, suffereth temptation, and yieldeth not to the temptation, but suffereth himself to be mocked, and scourged, and cast out, and disowned by his people. . . . Yea, even so he shall be led, crucified, and slain, the flesh becoming subject even unto death, the will of the Son being swallowed up in the will of the Father" (Mos. 15:1–5,7).

One student of the Book of Mormon, although recognizing

modalism in the passages cited above, has expressed caution about reaching that conclusion since there are "other passages which contradict the oneness demanded by modalism."[28] The passages to which he refers—the voice of the Father introducing the Son, the subjection of the Son unto the Father, the Son ascending to the Father (3 Ne. 11:6–8, 32; 15:1, 18–19; 18:27; 26:2, 5, 15)—all have parallels in the New Testament (Matt. 3:13–17; Jn. 14:28; 15:10; 16:28; 20:17). But such passages never dissuaded modalists. In view of the explicit modalistic passages in the Book of Mormon, the presence of apparent contradictions does not necessarily detract from a modalistic interpretation.[29]

A modalistic interpretation of the Book of Mormon fits well with other contemporary sources. In 1845 Lucy Smith recalled that shortly after the publication of the Book of Mormon, she had a discussion with some of her neighbors about the new scripture. During the conversation she "proceeded to relate the substance of what is contained in the book of Mormon, dwelling particularly upon the principles of religion therein contained." She also told the group that all the denominations were opposed to Mormonism and that the Methodists particularly "rage, for they worship a God without body or parts, and they know that our faith comes in contact with this principle."[30]

In context this statement does not mean that in 1830 Mormons were teaching that the Father has a body like the Son's—this concept was not introduced into Mormonism until much later. Nor does it necessarily imply that Lucy was reading a later Mormon concept into an earlier time. She was more likely contrasting the Book of Mormon's teaching that God the Father had become flesh with the orthodox creeds which distinguished between the persons of the Son and Father and described the Father as spirit essence. According to Lucy Smith, the Methodists thus objected to the Book of Mormon's modalistic view of God because it made the Father into a corporeal being.

Some of the revelations which Joseph Smith dictated between 1829 and 1831 similarly blur the distinction between the Father and the Son (D&C 11:2, 10, 28; 29:1, 42, 46; 49:5, 28).[31] Also in the early 1830s Smith revised the Bible, changing a number of passages to more explicitly identify the Son with the Father. For example, he changed Luke 10:22, in which Jesus declares that "no man knoweth who the Son is, but the Father; and who the Father is, but the Son, and he to whom the Son will reveal him." In the revised version Jesus says that "no man knoweth that the Son is the Father, and the Father is the Son, but him to whom the Son will reveal it."[32]

A public interpretation of the Book of Mormon's view of God appeared in an exchange of letters in 1837–38 between Mormon elder Stephen Post and Oliver Barr of the Christian Connection. The letters were published in the *Christian Palladium* (Union Mills, New York). Barr, a binitarian, criticized the Book of Mormon for not distinguishing between the person of the Father and the person of the Son. What Barr objected to most was the idea that the Father entered the world as Jesus and that Jesus was thus both Father and Son. It appalled Barr to think that "God the Creator, the Eternal Father had a mother; was a child, was born at Jerusalem, was spit upon, nailed to the cross, slain, and buried in a sepulchre."[33] "If the Father and Son are one person," Barr continued, "then part of his [Post's] God is *material!*" He concluded, "The Mormon God . . . [is] a complex, compound God!! part matter, part spirit, and yet eternal!"[34] Like the Methodists who confronted Lucy Smith in 1830, Barr attacked the book's modalistic view of God, especially its anthropomorphization of God the Father.

Barr did not confuse the Mormon view of God with orthodox trinitarianism. Rather he distinguished between the "triune God" of the Catholics and "another" God, "consisting of a Father, Son and a created tabernacle in which the Father and Son dwelt," which "Mormons have manufactured."[35] Barr did refer to the "Mormon Trinity," but as a binitarian he would have naturally classified most opposing views of the Godhead as trinitarian.[36] In Barr's view the Father and Son "were two distinct personages" but not "two Gods."[37] The Son is Lord and Savior but not God. The Father alone is God. "There is but one God the Father, and there is one Lord Jesus Christ, the Son of the Father," wrote Barr. "The Father is the *one* God, and Jesus Christ the Mediator *between* him and us."[38]

Post's task was to explain how "there is but one God" while at the same time maintaining that the Father is God and that the Son, as a separate personage, is also God.[39] Post quoted various scriptures to prove the view that the Son was merely "a personage of tabernacle" in which dwelt "all the fulness of the Father," that "the Godhead was concentrated in the Lord Jesus Christ, whose tabernacle contained

the fulness of the spirit of the everlasting God, the Almighty."[40]
Thus, according to Post, "Christ was not only God, possessing all the
fulness of the Father, he being the Father and the Father in him, he
and the Father being one; the Father because he gave the Son of his
fulness, and Son because he was in the world and made flesh his
tabernacle, and dwelt among the sons of men."[41] "The Father and
Son [were] united in the same person," and thus Jesus was literally
Father and Son.[42] The Father dwelling in Jesus "would truly be God
manifest in the flesh," Post concluded.[43]

    Post also attacked what he thought was Barr's bitheism, stat-
ing that if Jesus was more than "a personage of tabernacle," if the
Father and Son "were two distinct personages, with similar bodies
and minds ... [it] would assuredly make two Gods; whereas the
Scriptures plainly declare that there is but one."[44] Barr, however,
deflected this criticism by denying Jesus' deity, asserting that the
Father only was God.[45] The exchange is not only one example of how
Mormonism differed from other versions of Christian primitivism
but demonstrates the modalistic interpretation that some early Mormons placed on the Book of Mormon.[46]

    If the earliest Mormon concept of God was unlike orthodox
creeds, it also differed from what Joseph Smith later taught on the
subject. Various scholars have noticed a shift in the Mormon concept
of God in the mid-1830s. One writer, for example, remarked that
"revelations Joseph [Smith] received after 1833 contain less cross-
over in the roles and titles of the Father and the Son. In fact, it
appears that after May of 1833, Joseph never again referred to Jesus
as the Father in any of his writings."[47] Although the distinction
between the Father and Son initially was mostly implied in Mormon
theology, it was soon to become an express article of belief.

    What are commonly called the "Lectures on Faith" were
delivered at the School of the Elders in 1834 and were included in
all LDS editions of the Doctrine of Covenants between 1835 and
1921. These lectures described the Godhead as consisting of "two
personages": "the Father being a personage of spirit, ... the Son,
who was in the bosom of the Father, a personage of tabernacle, ...
possessing the same mind with the Father, which mind is the Holy
spirit, that bears record of the Father and the Son, and these three
are one."[48] Because the fifth lecture clearly distinguished between
the persons of the Father and Son but not the Holy Spirit, some have

concluded that this description of the Godhead represents a shift to binitarianism.[49]

Sidney Rigdon, an early Mormon convert from Campbellism, helped Joseph Smith prepare the lectures for publication. Consequently, the binitarian formulation of the Godhead in the lectures may reflect Rigdon's Primitivistic background.[50] In fact, several characteristics of the fifth lecture seem to reflect the "dynamic" monarchianism of the Christian Connection. The lecture never affirms the deity of Jesus but rather reflects a view expressed by Millard and other Primitivists that Jesus "possess[es] all the fulness of the Father ... being begotten of him," that he shares the divine nature through the "Holy Spirit," and that through the same Spirit the saints can become one with the Father "as the Father and Son are one." The lecture declares "salvation, through the atonement and mediation of Jesus Christ," but he is no longer the Father.[51] The lecture is consistent in its use of the term "Holy Spirit," a favorite with Campbell's movement, rather than the Mormon use of "Holy Ghost."

About the same time the lectures were being delivered, Joseph Smith's recitals of his first vision began to reflect the same view of the Godhead. In his 1832 history, Smith described only one personage appearing to him: "I saw the Lord [presumably Jesus Christ] and he spake unto me saying ... behold I am the Lord of glory I was crucifyed for the world."[52] This version was congruent with the Book of Mormon's theology. However, Edward Stevenson recalled hearing Smith describe to "large congregations" in 1834 "the visit of the Father and the Son, and the conversation he had with them."[53] When Smith related his experience in 1835, he not only said that "a personage appeared in the midst of [a] pillar of flame" but that "another personage soon appeared like unto the first."[54] After this Smith's recitals of his first vision — his 1838 history, his 1842 letter to John Wentworth, and various public statements — conformed to the definition of the Godhead outlined in the lectures.[55]

When Joseph Smith was preparing to publish a second edition of the Book of Mormon in 1837, he revised several passages to reflect this new understanding of the Godhead. Mary was no longer the "mother of God" but rather the "mother of *the Son of* God" (1 Ne. 11:18). Passages referring to Jesus as the "Eternal Father" and

"Everlasting God" were also modified with the addition of "Son of" (1 Ne. 11:21, 32; 13:40). Although these changes were not systematically made throughout the entire Book of Mormon, they nevertheless indicate that Mormon thinking had undergone revision.

If some Christians were unclear about the definition of the trinity, Mormons during the 1830s also held differing positions on the nature of God. It is probable, as some have suggested, that some early Mormon converts might have retained their former trinitarian views.[56] It is also probable, as has been suggested, that Sidney Rigdon and other Primitivists continued in their binitarianism. W. W. Phelps, for instance, recalled that even before his conversion to Mormonism, he had rejected trinitarianism and apparently saw no conflict between Mormonism and his belief "in God, and the Son of God, as two distinct characters."[57] Still others such as Stephen Post, apparently unaware of the shift in the mid-1830s, continued to defend the Book of Mormon's modalism. However, until clearly defined in the 1840s, the nature of God seems not to have been a major concern for most early Mormons, and shifts in teachings on the subject probably went unnoticed by the average member.

By the 1840s the Mormon concept of the Godhead had developed to a clearly defined tritheistic (literally, "three gods") position.[58] On 16 February 1841 Joseph Smith explained that "the Godhead . . . was Not as many imagined — three Heads & but one body, . . . [but rather] the three were separate bodys — God the first & Jesus the Mediator the 2d & the Holy Ghost & these three agree in one."[59] In September 1842 he further explained that "the Father, and the Son are persons of Tabernacle; and the Holy Ghost [is] a spirit." Also at this time he reportedly declared, "We believe in three Gods"[60] — a position he formulated in April 1843 into the following creed: "The Father has a body of flesh & bone as tangible as mans the Son also, but the Holy Ghost is a personage of spirit."[61]

Few subjects in Mormonism have been so affected by continuing revelation as the nature of God. Mormonism began with modalism, switched in the mid-1830s to a binitarian position similar to the Christian Connection, and finally moved in the early 1840s to tritheism. This shift — coupled with the related doctrine that in the universe there is a multitude of gods — eventually brought criticism upon the Mormon prophet from some of his own followers. On Sunday morning, 16 June 1844, amid accusations that he was a fallen

prophet because he had introduced "false and damnable doctrines ... such as plurality of Gods,"[62] Smith publicly declared: "I
have always and in all congregations when I have preached on the
subject of the Deity, it has been the plurality of Gods. It has been
preached by the Elders for fifteen years. I have always declared God
to be a distinct personage, Jesus Christ a separate and distinct personage from God the Father, and that the Holy Ghost was a distinct
personage and a Spirit: and these three constitute three distinct
personages and three Gods."[63]

Evidently not appreciating the fact that rhetoric and even
memory, especially during periods of crisis, may not always reflect
historical reality, some writers have tried to defend Smith's statement by harmonizing the Book of Mormon with Smith's later teachings.[64] However, the historical inaccuracies of the statement—the
most glaring of which concerns the Holy Ghost—should be apparent. The "Lectures on Faith" had declared that there were only "two
personages" in the Godhead—the Father and Son—the "Holy
Spirit" being "the Mind ... [and] the Spirit of the Father." Not until
the 1840s did Joseph Smith teach that the Holy Ghost was a
"personage" of spirit.[65] Also, while the Father was described in the
lectures as a personage of spirit, the Son was a personage of flesh
only and hence not separate from the Father. Moreover, the literal
oneness of the Book of Mormon's modalistic view of God precludes
Smith's claim that he had always taught that there were three Gods.

Although the earliest Mormon concept of God differed from
the belief Joseph Smith outlined in his sermons in the 1840s, later
Mormon theology does not trace its roots to trinitarianism or any
other orthodox creed. Rather Mormon theology consistently rejected orthodox definitions of God, developing in an increasingly
heterodox direction.

– NOTES –

1. *A Book of Commandments, for the Government of the Church of Christ*
(Zion [Independence, MO]: W. W. Phelps, 1833), 24:18. This passage was
altered in the 1835 edition of the Doctrine and Covenants (D&C): "Father,
Son, and Holy Ghost *are* one God" (20:28). On the dating of D&C 20, see
Lyndon W. Cook, *The Revelations of the Prophet Joseph Smith: A Historical and
Biographical Commentary of the Doctrine and Covenants* (Provo, UT: Seventy's
Mission Bookstore, 1981), 31.

2. On 19 April 1831, the *Painesville Telegraph* published D&C 20, referring to it as the "Mormon Creed."

3. Thomas G. Alexander, "The Reconstruction of Mormon Doctrine: From Joseph Smith to Progressive Theology," *Sunstone* 5 (July-Aug. 1980): 25. See also Boyd Kirkland, "Jehovah as the Father: The Development of the Mormon Jehovah Doctrine," *Sunstone* 9 (Autumn 1984): 37; Kirkland, "Elohim and Jehovah in Mormonism and the Bible," *Dialogue: A Journal of Mormon Thought* 19 (Spring 1986): 77; Van Hale, "Trinitarianism and the Earliest Mormon Concept of God," May 1983; and Gregory L. Kofford, "The First Vision: Doctrinal Development and Analysis," 1988. Van Hale, for example, has noted that "doctrinal development . . . was not simply an adding to, or expanding of early ideas, but also the weeding out of inconsistencies and the refining of both thought and terminology" (p. 13). Hale subsequently reconsidered his position on trinitarianism, stating that "Mormon doctrine has never been trinitarian" ("Defining the Mormon Doctrine of Deity," *Sunstone* 10 [Jan. 1985]: 27). Re-edited versions of Alexander's and Kirkland's essays appear in the present compilation.

4. *Millennial Harbinger*, Feb. 1831, 93.

5. Hosea Ballou, *A Treatise on Atonement* (Randolph, VT, 1805), 67.

6. For treatments of the primitive gospel movement and its affinity to early Mormonism, see Marvin S. Hill, "The Role of Christian Primitivism in the Origin and Development of the Mormon Kingdom, 1830-1844," Ph.D. diss., University of Chicago, 1968; Hill, "The Shaping of the Mormon Mind in New England and New York," *Brigham Young University Studies* 9 (Spring 1969): 351-72; and my *Religious Seekers and the Advent of Mormonism* (Salt Lake City: Signature Books, 1988).

7. John Rogers, *The Biography of Eld. Barton Warren Stone, Written by Himself: With Additions and Reflections*, 5th ed. (Cincinnati, 1847), 29.

8. In I. Daniel Rupp, comp., *He Pasa Ekklesia. An Original History of the Religious Denominations at Present Existing in the United States* (Philadelphia, 1844), 169.

9. David Millard, *The True Messiah* (Canandaigua, NY, 1823), 78-122.

10. James DeForest Murch, *Christians Only: A History of the Restoration Movement* (Cincinnati: Standard Publishing, 1962), 114-15. See also *Christian Palladium*, 1 Sept. 1837, 138-39; 15 Jan. 1838, 275.

11. See Van Hale, "Defining the Mormon Doctrine of Deity," 27.

12. Royal Humbert, ed., *A Compend of Alexander Campbell's Theology* (St. Louis: Bethany Press, 1961), 95.

13. *Millennial Harbinger*, 1833, 155.

14. See *Observer and Telegraph* [Hudson], 11 Nov. 1830, and 17 March 1831.

15. Humbert, *Compend of Alexander Campbell's Theology*, 116n4.

16. According to Dionysius, bishop of Rome in the mid-third century, in *The Ante-Nicene Fathers*, 10 vols. (Grand Rapids, MI: Eerdmans Publishing Co., 1975), 7:365. The third-century heretic Noetus also believed that "Christ was the Father Himself, and that the Father Himself was born, and suffered, and died" (5:223).

17. The example of the sun comes from Sabellius himself. See, for example, John McClintock and James Strong, eds., *Cyclopaedia of Biblical, Theological, and Ecclesiastical Literature* (New York: Harper & Brothers, 1894), 9:202. See also David Millard, *The True Messiah Exalted* (Canandaigua, NY, 1818), 36.

18. Millard, *True Messiah Exalted* (1818), 8.

19. Millard, *True Messiah* (1823), 36.

20. Lucy [Mack] Smith, *Biographical Sketches of Joseph Smith the Prophet, and His Progenitors for Many Generations* (Liverpool: S. W. Richards, 1853), 146.

21. See *Christian Palladium*, 16 Jan. 1837; 1 Sept. 1837; 15 Jan. 1838.

22. George B. Arbaugh, "Evolution of Mormon Doctrine," *Church History* 9 (June 1940), 158, 169; Robert N. Hullinger, *Mormon Answer to Skepticism: Why Joseph Smith Wrote the Book of Mormon* (St. Louis: Clayton Publishing House, 1980), 153.

23. The passage in 1 John 5:7 does not appear in any of the early manuscripts of the New Testament and is believed to have been added after the second century by advocates of trinitarianism. See George Arthur Buttrick, et al., *The Interpreter's Bible*, 12 vols. (New York: Abingdon Press, 1957), 12:293–94.

24. In addition, as Van Hale has pointed out, the Book of Mormon never describes the Godhead using trinitarian definitions such as three "persons" or one "substance" ("Trinitarianism and the Earliest Mormon Concept of God," 7).

25. This is also the conclusion of at least two other researchers: Hale, "Defining the Mormon Doctrine of Deity," 27; and Mark Thomas, "Scholarship and the Future of the Book of Mormon," *Sunstone* 5 (May-June 1980): 25, 26, 28n5.

26. Joseph Smith, Jr., *The Book of Mormon* (Palmyra, NY: E. B. Grandin, 1830), 25. This passage was changed in the 1837 edition to read "the mother of *the Son of* God" (1 Ne. 11:18).

27. Ibid. This passage was changed in the 1837 edition to read: "the Lamb of God, yea, even the *Son of the* Eternal Father" (1 Ne. 11:21).

28. Hale, "Defining the Mormon Doctrine of Deity," 27.

29. Boyd Kirkland has similarly argued that "the more specific Book of Mormon statements on the relationship between the Father and the

Son should serve as the framework for understanding the theology of 3 Nephi rather than vice-versa" ("Jehovah as Father," 43n7).

30. Smith, *Biographical Sketches*, 146.

31. See Kirkland, "Jehovah as the Father," 37.

32. Some have referred to Smith's revision of Genesis as evidence that as early as June 1830 he conceived the Father and Son as distinct persons in the Godhead (Moses 1:6; 2:26–27; 4:1–3). However, Smith's revision does not necessarily imply that there were two "personages" in the Godhead before the incarnation. Rather consider the following: "By the word of my power, have I created them [the inhabitants of earth], which is mine Only Begotten Son" (Moses 1:32). See also Alexander's discussion in "Reconstruction of Mormon Doctrine," 33n23.

33. *Christian Palladium*, 16 Jan. 1837, 275; 1 Sept. 1837, 138.

34. Ibid., 15 Jan. 1838, 275.

35. Ibid., 1 Sept. 1837, 139.

36. *Christian Palladium*, 15 Jan. 1838, 275. David Millard, for instance, described modalists as "Trinitarians" (*True Messiah Exalted* [1818], 8).

37. *Christian Palladium*, 15 Jan. 1838, 275.

38. Ibid.; compare 1 Cor. 8:6; Eph. 4:5–6; 1 Tim. 2:5.

39. Ibid., 1 Aug. 1837, 99.

40. Ibid., 1 Aug. 1837, 99; 1 Dec. 1837, 230; compare Eph. 1:23; Col. 1:19; 2:9.

41. Ibid., 1 Aug. 1837, 99.

42. Ibid., 1 Aug. 1837, 99; 1 Dec. 1837, 230.

43. Ibid., 1 Aug. 1837, 99; compare 1 Tim. 3:16.

44. Ibid., 1 Dec. 1837, 230.

45. Ibid., 15 Jan. 1838, 275.

46. For differences between early Mormonism and other primitive gospel movements, see Vogel, *Religious Seekers*.

47. Kirkland, "Jehovah as the Father," 37.

48. Joseph Smith, Jr., et al., *Doctrine and Covenants of the Church of the Latter Day Saints: Carefully Selected From the Revelations of God* (Kirtland, OH: Printed by F. G. Williams & Co., 1835), 52–53.

49. Hale, "Defining the Mormon Doctrine of Deity," 26; Kirkland, "Jehovah as the Father," 37.

50. Evidence for Rigdon's possible influence on the "Lectures on Faith" has been considered in Leland H. Gentry, "What of the Lectures on Faith?" *Brigham Young University Studies* 19 (Fall 1978): 13–19.

51. Smith, *Doctrine and Covenants*, 53–54.

52. Dean C. Jessee, ed., *The Personal Writings of Joseph Smith* (Salt Lake City: Deseret Book, 1984), 6; compare Scott H. Faulring, ed., *An American*

Prophet's Record: The Diaries and Journals of Joseph Smith (Salt Lake City: Signature Books, 1987), 5-6.

53. Edward Stevenson, *Reminiscences of Joseph, The Prophet, and the Coming Forth of the Book of Mormon* (Salt Lake City, 1893), 4.

54. Milton V. Backman, Jr., *Joseph Smith's First Vision: Confirming Evidences and Contemporary Accounts*, 2d ed. (Salt Lake City: Bookcraft, 1980), 159.

55. For various accounts of the first vision, see ibid., 155-81.

56. Hale, "Trinitarianism and the Earliest Mormon Concept of God," 16; Kofford, "The First Vision," 16.

57. *Messenger and Advocate*, April 1835, 1:115, quoted in Robert L. Millet, *"To Be Learned Is Good If . . . ": A Response by Mormon Educators to Controversial Religious Questions* (Salt Lake City: Bookcraft, 1987), 70.

58. Hale, "Defining the Mormon Doctrine of Deity," 25.

59. In Andrew F. Ehat and Lyndon W. Cook, comps. and eds., *The Words of Joseph Smith: The Contemporary Accounts of the Nauvoo Discourses of the Prophet Joseph* (Salt Lake City: Bookcraft, 1980), 63.

60. *Time and Seasons*, 15 Sept. 1842, 926. Although this article appears under Smith's editorship, it is not certain he authored it. Apostle John Taylor was also doing some of the editing at this time.

61. In Ehat and Cook, 173, 268-69n5; see also Faulring, 341; D&C 130:22.

62. *Nauvoo Expositor*, 7 June 1844, 2.

63. Joseph Smith, Jr., et al., *History of the Church of Jesus Christ of Latter-day Saints*, ed. B. H. Roberts, 7 vols., 2nd rev. ed. (Salt Lake City: Deseret Book, 1964), 6:474; compare Ehat and Cook, 378.

64. Millet, *"To Be Learned Is Good If . . . ,"* 73.

65. Ehat and Cook, 63; *Times and Seasons*, 15 Sept. 1842, 926.

4.
The Development of the Mormon Doctrine of God

Boyd Kirkland

TODAY IN MORMON THEOLOGY JESUS CHRIST IS BELIEVED TO BE Jehovah, God of the Old Testament, while Elohim is God the Father, father of Jehovah and the entire human race. The LDS church promotes these ideas in its lesson manuals, periodicals, and literature.[1]

Although it might be natural to assume that this has always been the position of Mormonism, Mormon perceptions about God have passed through several phases of development.[2] Joseph Smith's earliest statements and scriptural writings describe God as an absolute, infinite, self-existent, spiritual being, perfect in all of his attributes and alone in his supremacy.[3] The Godhead was regularly defined with the trinitarian but nonbiblical formula, "the Father, Son, and Holy Ghost, which is one God."[4] The Book of Mormon speaks of only one god, who could manifest himself either as the Father or the Son.[5] Although Book of Mormon modalistic theology does not reflect a truly orthodox trinitarian view, it does reflect the Protestant primitivist perception that in some manner the Father and the Son were both representations of the one God.[6]

Several scriptural passages given through Smith indicate clearly that he saw no contradiction in having one god simultaneously be the Father who sent Jesus as well as Jesus himself.[7] For example, Ether 4:12 in the Book of Mormon plainly states, "He that will not believe me will not believe the Father who sent me. For behold, I am the Father."

A close examination of Joseph Smith's translation of the

35

Bible (JST) also reveals his early monotheistic beliefs. Smith consciously attempted to remove all references to a plurality of gods
from the King James Bible (KJV).[8] He also changed several passages
to identify more clearly the Father and the Son as the same god. For
example, he revised Luke 10:22 (in JST) to have Jesus teach that "no
man knoweth that the Son is the Father, and the Father is the Son,
but him to whom the Son will reveal it." These observations provide
significant insight into understanding Book of Mormon passages
which identify Jesus Christ as "God Himself," the "Holy One of
Israel," the "Lord Omnipotent," the "Father of heaven and earth"
who revealed himself to Moses and many of the ancient patriarchs.
Apparently Smith's own early theology is reflected in his translation
of the Book of Mormon. Similarly, some of Smith's early revelations
freely switch the role of the God of Israel from the Son to the
Father.[9]

    Evidence indicates that by 1835, Smith and other Mormon
leaders had begun to distinguish more between the roles and natures of the Father and the Son. This is reflected most clearly in the
"Lectures on Faith" published in the 1835 edition of the Doctrine
and Covenants. The fifth lecture defined the Godhead as consisting
of two personages: the Father, a personage of spirit, and the Son, a
personage of tabernacle. The Holy Ghost was not considered a personage but rather was defined as the "mind" of the Father and the
Son. Also, revelations Smith received after 1833 contain less cross-
over in the roles and titles of the Father and the Son. It is significant
that after May 1833 Smith apparently never again referred to Jesus as
the Father in any of his writings.

    Prior to his study of Hebrew in Kirtland, Ohio, Smith's us-
age of Elohim and Jehovah reflects marked similarity to the King
James Bible's usage of these names. Elohim and Jehovah appear
thousands of times in the original Hebrew Bible. However, they are
generally translated as "God" and "LORD" in the KJV, Jehovah appearing untranslated only six times in the KJV, while Elohim does
not appear at all. Accordingly, Jehovah appears in the Book of Mormon only twice, one reference being an excerpt from Isaiah. The
name Elohim appears nowhere in the LDS standard works: the Bible, the Book of Mormon, the Doctrine and Covenants, and the Pearl
of Great Price.

    After Smith's study of Hebrew in 1835–36, he began to use

Elohim for the first time; he also began to use Jehovah more often. Jehovah appears for the first time in the Doctrine and Covenants after 1836. It appears twice in the first two chapters of the "Book of Abraham," which were translated in 1835 and later published as part of the Pearl of Great Price.

Given the interchangeability of the roles of the Father and the Son in earliest Mormon theology, it is impossible to identify specifically Smith's first few Jehovah references as applying to either the Father or the Son. However, after the identities of the Father and the Son were more carefully differentiated around 1835, Smith clearly began to use the divine name Jehovah to refer to the Father. Significantly, he never seems to have specifically identified Jehovah as Jesus, nor Jehovah as the Son of Elohim. Rather, he followed the biblical Hebrew usage of the divine names in specific verses and either combined them or used them interchangeably as epithets for God the Father. The following prayer, which he wrote in 1842, demonstrates this: "O Thou, who seest and Knowest the hearts of all men — Thou eternal, omnipotent, omniscient, and omnipresent Jehovah — God — Thou Elohim, that sittest, as saith the Psalmist, 'enthroned in heaven,' look down upon Thy servant Joseph at this time; and let faith on the name of Thy Son Jesus Christ, to a greater degree than Thy servant ever yet has enjoyed, be conferred upon him."[10] On a few occasions, Smith referred to the Father by the title Elohim alone.[11]

Other Mormon writers during the 1830s followed this pattern, often using Jehovah as the name of God the Father and only occasionally using the name Elohim. However, they evidently considered the Father to be the god who appeared in the Old Testament. For example, the following was published in the *Times and Seasons* as the Mormon belief in 1841: "We believe in God the Father, who is the Great Jehovah and head of all things, and that Christ is the Son of God, co-eternal with the Father."[12]

During the Nauvoo, Illinois, period of church history (1839–44), Smith's theology of the Godhead once again changed dramatically. He began to denounce and reject the notion of the trinity altogether. He emphasized that God the Father, as well as the Son, both had tangible bodies of flesh and bone (D&C 130:22). He also began to teach the plurality of gods and the related concept that humans could become gods. God himself had a father upon whom he depended for his existence and authority. The Father had acted under the direction of a "head god" and a "council of gods" in the creation of the worlds. The plurality of creation gods was dramatically depicted in the "Book of Abraham," chapters 2–5, which Smith translated in 1842. All of these ideas were summed up by Smith in April 1844 in perhaps his most famous sermon, the King Follett Discourse.

In connection with these ideas, Smith began to use the title Elohim as the proper name for the head god who presided at the creation of the world. He also taught that Elohim in the creation accounts of Genesis should be understood in a plural sense as referring to the council of the gods, who, under the direction of the head god, organized the heavens and the earth. Once the earth had been organized, "the heads of the Gods appointed one God for us."[13] From the context of Smith's discussions of this head god, it is apparent that he considered this being to be a patriarchal superior to the father of Jesus.

The gods involved in the creation were designated in Smith's temple endowment ceremony as Elohim, Jehovah, and Michael. Smith had previously identified Michael as "Adam . . . the ancient of days" (D&C 27:11). Whether he identified either this Elohim or Jehovah to be God the Father as he had previously used these titles is unclear. We have seen that he used the title Elohim in various modes, none of which included Jesus, and he also used the name Jehovah to refer to the Father. Given all of these possibilities, Smith's endowment ceremony, then, did not seem to include Jesus among the creation gods. This is a curious situation, since many scriptural passages previously produced through Smith, as well as the Bible, attribute a major role in the creation to Jesus.[14] The inclusion of Michael was an interesting addition to the temple creation narrative, as he is not given a role in any of the scriptural creation accounts. Unfortunately, Smith was killed before he was able to elaborate further on these newer ideas.

As Smith's successor and devoted disciple, Brigham Young continued to teach Smith's Nauvoo theology to the church. On numerous occasions he clearly designated the God of the Old Testament as the Father[15] and delighted in citing the theophanies of the Old Testament as evidence of the Father's physical, anthropomorphic nature.[16] He likewise sometimes combined the names

Elohim-Jehovah or used them interchangeably as designations for God the Father: "We obey the Lord, Him who is called Jehovah, the Great I Am, I am a man of war, Elohim, etc."[17]

But if Young used these names interchangeably, how did he perceive the identities of Jehovah and Elohim in the temple cere-mony? This question can be answered by examining his teachings concerning Michael, the third figure in this creation story. Signifi-cantly, Young considered Michael, or Adam, to be God the Father — a belief extremely well documented.[18] For example, in one of his less ambiguous statements concerning his belief about the paternity of Jesus, Young said, "Who did beget him? . . . His Father; and his Father is our God, and the Father of our spirits, and he is the framer of the body, the God and Father of Our Lord Jesus Christ. Who is he? He is Father Adam; Michael; the Ancient of Days."[19]

The fact that Elohim and Jehovah preside over Michael in the temple creation account implies that, in this context at least, Young considered the pair to be patriarchal superiors to God the Father. Like Smith, then, Young apparently did not see Jesus as one of the temple creation gods. Perhaps this is explained by Young's belief that only a resurrected being can handle matter and create, although Young also referred at times to Jesus' role as a creator as mentioned in the scriptures. References indicating who exactly Young did consider this Elohim and Jehovah to be, and their rela-tionship to Michael-Adam, are sparse and ambiguous. However, the temple scenario depicts Elohim as the father of Adam and Eve. This coincides with Young's designation of Elohim as the grandfather of humankind. It is also consistent with Smith's teaching that the Creation was directed by a head god superior to our Father in Heaven.[20]

Since Young considered the Father to be Adam, and since he consistently designated the God of the Old Testament to be the Father, it is logical to suppose that he believed Adam to be the God of Israel. Indeed, on several occasions, he implied that this was the case: "The father of our Lord Jesus Christ, and of our spirits . . . [is] that great and wise and glorious being that the children of Israel were afraid of, whose countenance shown so that they could not look upon him . . . I tell you this as my belief about the personage who is called the Ancient of Days, the Prince, and so on."[21] In General Conference, 8 October 1854, Young specifically applied the title

Jehovah to Adam, calling him "Yahovah Michael," who carried out the behests of Elohim in the creation of the world.[22]

Young apparently believed that while God the Father was on the earth in the role of Adam, Elohim (the Grandfather in Heaven) assumed Adam's role as the Father of humankind. After his death, Adam returned to his exalted station as God the Father, and as such presided over Israel designated by the divine names Elohim or Jehovah. He later begot Jesus, his firstborn spirit son, in the flesh.

Thus a certain flexibility characterizes the way Young used the divine names. First, he never referred to Jesus as Jehovah. Second, he referred to God the Father variously as Jehovah, Elohim, Michael, Adam, Ancient of Days, I Am, and other Old Testament epithets. Finally, he also referred to gods superior to the Father as Elohim and Jehovah. Young's application of the titles Elohim and Jehovah to several different divine personalities has led to much confusion in understanding his true beliefs, especially with respect to the Adam-God doctrine.

Scriptures apparently contradicting the Adam-God doctrine, such as the accounts of Adam's creation, were dismissed by Young as "baby stories" given to people because of their spiritual immaturity and weakness.[23] During a discussion of the Adam-God doctrine at the Salt Lake City School of the Prophets, Young responded to the question of "why the scriptures seemed to put Jesus Christ on an equal footing with the Father" (presumably a reference to Book of Mormon theology). He explained that "the writers of those scriptures wrote according to their best language and understanding,"[24] indicating that Young did not feel obligated to accept literally all scriptural accounts of the role of Christ.

While not all General Authorities contemporary with and succeeding Young agreed with his teachings concerning Michael, many of them did speak of Jehovah as the Father. John Taylor consistently did so in numerous sermons, as well as in his book, *The Mediation and Atonement*, which he wrote as president of the church.[25] The following hymn, written by Taylor, clearly identifies Jehovah as the Father: "As in the heavens they all agree/ The record's given there by three, . . . / Jehovah, God the Father's one,/ Another His Eternal Son,/ The Spirit does with them agree,/ The witnesses in heaven are three."[26]

In some 256 references to Elohim and Jehovah and the God

of the Old Testament in the *Journal of Discourses* (representing ser-
mons of many of the First Presidency and Quorum of the Twelve
Apostles), the title Jehovah is only specifically applied to Jesus once.
This occurred in 1885 when the new doctrine identifying Jesus as
Jehovah was just beginning to be developed.

Not surprisingly, some confusion arose among Mormons
who had trouble reconciling their reading of the scriptures with
Smith's and Young's later doctrinal innovations. For example, the
Book of Mormon's explicit identification of Jesus as God the Father
led some members to believe that Jesus was literally the father of
the spirits of humankind. This, coupled with Young's Adam-God
doctrine, apparently led others to identify Adam and Christ as the
same being. Also, because of the Book of Mormon's equating of Jesus
with the God of Israel, some General Authorities in the 1880s and
1890s began to speculate that *all* Old Testament appearances and
revelations of God were in reality manifestations of the premortal
Jesus. This concept eventually led to the identification of Jesus as
Jehovah.

As early as 1849, Apostle Orson Pratt observed that there
were "some [Saints] . . . who believed that the spirit of Christ, before
taking a tabernacle, was the Father, exclusively of any other being.
They suppose the fleshly tabernacle to be the Son, and the Spirit
who came and dwelt in it to be the Father; hence they suppose the
Father and Son were united in *one* person, and that when Jesus dwelt
on the earth in the flesh, they suppose there was no distinct separate
person from himself who was called the Father."

This was apparently a Book-of-Mormon-influenced idea
which Pratt resolved by demonstrating from other scriptures (mostly
biblical) that the Father and Son were two separate personages. As
part of his harmonizing technique, Pratt qualified the sense in which
Jesus is called the Father in the Book of Mormon. Interestingly,
however, he still referred to God the Father as Jehovah in this same
presentation.[27]

Apostle George Q. Cannon was one of the first Mormon
leaders to assert that Jesus was "the Being who spoke to Moses in the
wilderness and declared, 'I am that I am.' "[28] Eleven years after this
1871 declaration, Apostle Franklin D. Richards also identified Jesus
Christ as "the same being who called Abraham from his native coun-
try, who led Israel out of the land of Egypt . . . and who made known

to them his law amid the thunderings of Sinai."[29] Furthermore, John Taylor, who throughout his life consistently referred to the Father as Jehovah, listed Jehovah among several other titles of the Father which might be applied to Jesus, since Jesus was perfectly obedient to and united with the Father.[30]

In August 1885, Franklin D. Richards made the leap from merely considering Jesus to be Jehovah's representative (and thus worthy of the latter's title) to the position that Jesus' premortal name was Jehovah: "We learn that our Savior was born of a woman, and He was named Jesus the Christ. His name when He was a spiritual being, during the first half of the existence of the earth, before He was made flesh and blood, was Jehovah. . . . He was the spirit Being that directed, governed, and gave the law on Mount Sinai, where Moses was permitted to see Him in part."[31] That this was a new idea is indicated by the fact that just four months prior to this sermon, Richards had also spoken of Jehovah as the Father.[32]

At these early stages of the development of the Jehovah-Christ doctrine, the major consideration seemed to be the identity of the divine being who appeared to Moses and gave him the law for Israel (compare 3 Ne. 15:5). The Adam-God doctrine, with its concept of a divine being named Jehovah who presided over God the Father (Michael-Adam) in the Creation, was not a consideration. This is indicated by the fact that both George Q. Cannon and Franklin D. Richards, major proponents of the Jehovah-Christ idea, also believed that Adam was God the Father.[33] In June 1889 Cannon, then a member of the First Presidency, related his beliefs on the Adam-God doctrine as well as the Jehovah-Christ doctrine to his son, Abraham, who wrote in his diary, "He believes that Jesus Christ is Jehovah, and that Adam is His Father and our God. . . . Jesus, in speaking of Himself as the very eternal Father speaks as one of the Godhead, etc."[34]

It is unclear whether Cannon and Richards considered the Jehovah of the temple ceremony to be Christ. They both, however, positively believed that Jehovah, the God of the Old Testament, was Christ, which they continued to teach on several occasions.[35]

The identities and roles of the temple creation gods became the focus of a controversy between Bishop Edward Bunker and his counselor Myron Abbott in Bunkerville, Nevada, in 1890. This controversy culminated in 1892 in a St. George, Utah, stake high council meeting attended by church president Wilford Woodruff and his counselor George Q. Cannon. Bunker and his father, Edward Sr., felt that the "Lecture before the Veil," as it was then presented in the St. George Temple, contained false doctrine.

This veil lecture, dictated by Brigham Young in 1877, clearly implied that Adam was God the Father by explaining that prior to coming to this earth, Adam and Eve had been resurrected and exalted on a former world. In their exalted state they begot the spirits of all humankind. Under the direction of Elohim and Jehovah, gods of the creation council, Adam then created this earth and brought Eve here with him to fall in order to provide their spiritual offspring with physical tabernacles.[36] The Bunkers maintained that these ideas contradicted the scriptures and Joseph Smith's teachings. The elder Bunker also argued that Jesus Christ was Jehovah, the God of heaven, who presided over Michael in the Creation and in the Garden of Eden. According to this argument, Michael could not possibly be the father of Christ since he was subject to Jehovah-Christ whom Bunker apparently also considered to be the Father.[37]

Presidents Woodruff and Cannon defended Brigham Young's Adam-God temple teachings but did not expound upon them or force them upon the Bunkers. Rather, they instructed them to "let these things alone" and not to "spend time [arguing] over these mysteries." Scriptural contradictions to these ideas were swept aside by Cannon with the observation that "God, had, and would yet reveal many glorious things men could not prove, and search out of the old Bible."[38]

As a counselor to Woodruff, Cannon preached that Jesus was Jehovah. Woodruff, however, was more noncommittal. As late as 1893, he still referred to Jehovah as the Father.[39] Latter-day Saints were thus confronted with an array of different authorities on the question of God's identity and roles. Apparently, many of these members wrote letters to the First Presidency, asking for help in sorting out and understanding these matters. President Woodruff responded to these inquiries over the pulpit at General Conference in April 1895 by simply telling church members not to worry about it. Interestingly, he too remained noncommittal, neither condemning the Adam-God doctrine nor endorsing the Jehovah-Christ doctrine: "Cease troubling yourselves about who God is; who Adam is, who Christ is, who Jehovah is. . . . God is God. Christ is Christ. The

Holy Ghost is the Holy Ghost. That should be enough for you and me to know."[40]

Not surprisingly, Woodruff's advice did not end the controversy. Edward Stevenson, one of the seven presidents of the Seventy, also was interested in sorting out the identities of the temple creation gods, and in 1896 he had "a deep talk" with President Lorenzo Snow about the Adam-God doctrine. Stevenson recorded his personal beliefs in his diary: "Certainly Heloheim and Jehovah stands before Adam, or else I am very much mistaken. Then 1st Heloheim, 2nd Jehovah, 3d Michael-Adam, 4th Jesus Christ, Our Elder Brother, in the other World from whence our spirits come. . . . Then Who is Jehovah? The only begoton Son of Heloheim on Jehovah's world."[41]

This reference clearly distinguishes between Jehovah, who presided over Michael at the Creation, and Jesus. Unfortunately, this distinction was not clearly made by General Authorities who were publicly promoting the idea that Jesus was the Jehovah-god of the Old Testament. Naturally, church members continued to be confused.

With the passing of the Mormon practice of plural marriage around the turn of the twentieth century, anti-Mormon critics began to attack other doctrinal issues, notably the Adam-God doctrine.[42] Church leaders responded mainly by claiming that Brigham Young's published statements on the subject had either been misinterpreted or wrongly transcribed.[43] President Joseph F. Smith, who as an apostle had earlier endorsed the doctrine, permitted Charles Penrose, his counselor in the First Presidency, to pursue this line of defense.[44]

While General Authorities had previously asserted that the Adam-God doctrine need not be justified scripturally, the First Presidency now moved to abate public criticism and internal controversy by citing the scriptures as the final, official word on the matter. For example, in 1912, they stated, "Dogmatic assertions do not take the place of revelation," and that "Prest. Brigham Young . . . only expressed his own views and that they were not corobirated [sic] by the word of the Lord in the Standard Works of the Church. . . . Now all doctrine if it can't be established by these standards is not to be taught or promolgated by members."[45]

At the same time, the *Improvement Era* carried a First Presidency message cautioning members not to speculate on "the career of Adam before he came to the earth." This was followed by an editorial responding to members who apparently considered Christ and Adam to be the same god: "From these statements, and from many others that might be quoted, it is clear that Adam and Christ are two persons—not the same person. It is erroneous doctrine to consider them one and the same person, for Jesus is the Christ, a member of the Trinity, the Godhead, and to whom Adam, the father of the human family upon this earth is amenable."[46] Many statements similar to this followed in church publications.[47]

A major advance in identifying Jehovah as Jesus took place in September 1915 when Apostle James E. Talmage's book *Jesus the Christ* was published under the direction of the First Presidency. In his book, Talmage asserted that "Jesus Christ was and is God the Creator, . . . the God of the Old Testament record; and the God of the Nephites. We affirm that Jesus Christ was and is Jehovah, the Eternal One." He also explained that "*Elohim*, as understood and used in the restored Church of Jesus Christ, is the name-title of God the Eternal Father, whose firstborn Son in the spirit is Jehovah—the Only Begotten in the flesh, Jesus Christ." A subtle rejection of Brigham Young's Adam-God doctrine seems to be present in Talmage's assertion that Adam was one of the prophets to whom the Father revealed himself to attest to "the Godship of the Christ."[48]

Members of the First Presidency continued to reinforce these ideas in conference talks and church publications.[49] In addition to accommodating Book of Mormon theology (which described Jesus as the God of Israel), defining Jehovah exclusively to be Jesus and Elohim exclusively to be God the Father permitted church leaders to argue more effectively that the Adam-God doctrine—at least as it was popularly understood—could never have been taught. The thrust of this argument was that since Elohim was the Father and Jehovah was Jesus, and since they both presided over Michael or Adam in the Creation, Brigham Young could not possibly have meant that Adam was God the Father.[50]

This argument was effective, but it obviously would not suffice for church members who had heard Young publicly preach the Adam-God doctrine, had read his sermons on the subject, or had witnessed the temple lecture he authored. As a result, many members continued to write to the First Presidency, apparently protesting their efforts via Charles Penrose and James Talmage to redefine the theological views of previous Mormon leaders. Penrose referred to this resistance in his April 1916 General Conference address: "I frequently personally receive letters from good friends in different parts of the Church, asking questions, and declaring that there is a division of opinion among our brethren in regard to them. . . . There still remains, I can tell by the letters I have alluded to, an idea among some of the people that Adam was and is the Almighty and Eternal God." Penrose also noted that some members still believed that Jesus and Adam were the same god. He responded to these issues by combining the newly developed theology of Elohim as the Father and Jesus as Jehovah with the temple account of the Creation to refute the Adam-God doctrine: "We are told by revelation that in the creation of the earth there were three individuals personally engaged. This is more particularly for the Temple of God, but sufficient of it has been published over and over again to permit me to refer to it. [The title] Elohim . . . is attached to the individual who is the Father of all, the person whom we look to as the Great Eternal Father. Elohim, Jehovah and Michael were engaged in the construction of this globe. Jehovah, commanded by Elohim, went down to where there was space, saying to Michael, 'Let us go down.' . . . You see, do you not, that Michael became Adam, and that Adam was not the son Jehovah, and he was not Elohim the Father. He occupied his own place and position in the organization of the earth and in the production of mortal beings on the earth. Jesus of Nazareth was the Jehovah who was engaged with the Father in the beginning . . . I want to draw a clear distinction between these individuals that we may stop this discussion that is going on to no purpose."[51]

The theological problems concerning the Book of Mormon's identification of Jesus as the Father, the identity of Jehovah, the God of Israel, and the roles and identities of the temple creation gods as connected with the Adam-God doctrine were all finally "resolved" in a carefully worked-out statement by Talmage. This statement was submitted to the First Presidency and the Council of the Twelve Apostles for their approval on 29 June 1916. It was corrected and then issued the following day as "A Doctrinal Exposition by the First Presidency and the Twelve" on "The Father and the Son."[52]

This exposition minimized through harmonizing techniques the sense in which Jesus is called the Father in the Book of Mormon. It also supported the position that Jesus Christ was

Jehovah, the God of Israel, and that Elohim was his father. Little biblical support for these ideas could be given, as the exposition mainly dealt with problems inherent in early LDS scriptures and the theology of Joseph Smith and Brigham Young. Achieving harmony was the chief goal of the 1916 doctrinal exposition. It therefore contains no historical analysis of the problems it addresses. Its definitions of Elohim and Jehovah remain the official position of Mormonism.

Despite the attempt at harmonization, the current Mormon definitions of Elohim and Jehovah and identification of Jesus as the God of Israel—like Brigham Young's earlier teachings, ironically— do not seem to accord with the biblical record.[53] Efforts of some Mormon writers to harmonize these definitions with the Bible have led to misunderstanding and manipulation of the scriptures. For example, biblical passages which refer to Jehovah in the context of being the Father have been interpreted to refer to Elohim.[54] Scriptural prayers addressed to Jehovah have been diluted with the interpretation that they are mere exclamations of joy, worship, and adoration to our Savior rather than true prayers addressed to God the Father.[55] This interpretation has been made necessary by the Mormon belief that all true worship and prayer should be directed to God the Father, not to the Son.[56] But if Jesus was literally Jehovah, the God of Israel, then the Israelites were indeed worshipping and praying to the Son to the exclusion of the Father. One Mormon writer, commenting on this dilemma, observed, "When Christ was on the earth he taught his disciples to worship the Father. It doesn't seem logical to me that Christ would ask in the Old Testament to be worshipped, and not have the Father worshipped as in other scriptures, in other dispensations . . . [The] Jews and their Old Testament ancestors considered Elohim and Jehovah to be two names for God which both refer to a single deity . . . "[57]

Furthermore, biblical messianic prophesies in which the Messiah is obviously described as the servant of Jehovah have been misunderstood or reinterpreted.[58] Titles of Jehovah such as "Savior," "Redeemer of Israel," etc., have been isolated from their Old Testament context in efforts to promote the Jehovah/Christ idea.[59] The "divine investiture" harmonizing concept (where the Son speaks and acts in the first person as if he were the Father) has been used whenever the scriptures have God making appearances and giving revelations. This has been made necessary because of the current Mormon concept that all revelation since the fall of Adam has come through the Son.[60] Interestingly, however, these same scriptural passages are sometimes cited in Mormonism as evidence of the Father's physical, anthropomorphic nature.[61]

Some Mormon writers aware of these problems have concluded that the entire biblical record as we now have it has been so systematically corrupted and edited through the centuries that all indications of a theology more in conformity with current Mormon definitions have been obliterated.[62] Modern textual criticism and comparisons of the many available ancient manuscripts of the Bible do not lend much support to such a radical thesis. Likewise, efforts to show parallels between Mormonism and the polytheism of the patriarchal era also seem misdirected.[63] This approach is similar to the "parallelomania" which intrigued many LDS church members during the late 1960s and early 1970s with the publication of the Dead Sea Scrolls and the Nag Hammadi gnostic texts. Parallels between Mormonism and ancient Near Eastern theologies seem to exist superficially, but when these parallels are returned to their original context, their significance greatly diminishes if not disappears. The vast majority of the theology, mythology, and religious practices of the various ancient groups cited in these "parallel" comparisons would shock and confound most contemporary Mormons.

Today, Mormons who are aware of the various teachings of LDS scriptures and prophets over the years are faced with a number of doctrinal possibilities. They can choose to accept Book of Mormon theology, but this varies from biblical theology as well as from Joseph Smith's later plurality-of-gods theology. There is Brigham Young's Adam-God theology with its various gods using the names Elohim and Jehovah interchangeably, but this finds little "official" support today. Or they can try to resolve the teachings of current General Authorities who identify Jesus as Jehovah with nineteenth-century General Authorities who spoke of Jehovah as the Father. While most Mormons are unaware of the diversity that abounds in the history of Mormon doctrine, many Latter-day Saints since 1916 have, despite the risk of heresy, continued to believe or promote publicly many of the alternative Godhead theologies from Mormonism's past.

– NOTES –

1. See, for example, Bruce R. McConkie, "Christ and the Creation," *Ensign* 12 (June 1982): 11; *Old Testament Part Two: Gospel Doctrine Teacher's Supplement* (Salt Lake City: Church of Jesus Christ of Latter-day Saints, 1980), 102–105; *Old Testament: Genesis-2 Samuel* [Religion 301 student manual] (Salt Lake City: LDS Church Educational System, 1980), 45–48.

2. See Thomas G. Alexander, "The Reconstruction of Mormon Doctrine: From Joseph Smith to Progressive Theology," *Sunstone* 5 (July-Aug. 1980): 24–33; Van Hale, "The Doctrinal Impact of the King Follett Discourse," *Brigham Young University Studies* 18 (Winter 1978): 215–16, and "Trinitarianism and the Earliest Mormon Concept of God," essay presented at Mormon History Association annual meeting, May 1983; Marvin S. Hill, "The First Vision Controversy: A Critique and a Reconciliation," *Dialogue: A Journal of Mormon Thought* 15 (Summer 1982): 31–46; Mark Thomas, "Scholarship and the Future of the Book of Mormon," *Sunstone* 5 (May-June 1980): 25–26, 28n5.

3. See, for example, in the Book of Mormon: 1 Ne. 10:18–19; 2 Ne. 9:20; Al. 18:18, 28; 22:9–11; 26:35; Morm. 9:9, 17, 19; Moro. 7:22; 8:18; in the D&C: 20:17, 28; 38:1–3; 76:1–4,70; or in the Pearl of Great Price: Moses 1:3, 6.

4. 2 Ne. 31:21; Mos. 15:4; Al. 11:44; 3 Ne. 11:27, 36; 28:10–11; Morm. 7:7; D&C 20:27–28. The only passage in the Bible containing the formula, "The Father, the Word, and the Holy Spirit, and these three are one" (1 John 5:7) is not found in any of the most ancient manuscripts or in the writings of the early church fathers. All modern critical translations of the New Testament omit the passage. Thus its presence in the Book of Mormon seems to be an anomaly.

5. Book of Mormon, 1830 ed., 1 Ne. 11:21, 28; in current editions, see Mos. 3:5–8; 7:27; 15:1–5; Al. 11:28, 29, 38, 39, 44; 3 Ne. 1:14; Morm. 5:17; 9:9–12; Eth. 3:14f; 4:12.

6. See Hale, "Earliest Mormon Concept of God," 5, 7–8, 12–13; and Dan Vogel, "The Earliest Mormon Concept of God," in this volume.

7. See Eth. 4:12; 2 Ne. 11:7; 3 Ne. 1:14; Moses 7:50f; JST, Luke 10:22.

8. Compare, for example, the JST's revisions of the following KJV passages: Gen. 11:7; Ex. 7:1; 22:28; 1 Sam. 28:13; Matt. 9:15–16; 11:27; Mark 2:28; Luke 10:22; 1 Tim. 2:4; Rev. 1:6.

9. D&C 1:20; 6:2, 21; 11:2, 10, 28; 14:2, 9; 17:9; 18:33, 47; 19:1, 4, 10, 16, 18; 27:1; 29:1, 42, 46; 34:1–4; 38:1–4; 49:5, 28; etc.; Book of Mormon, 1830 ed., 1 Ne. 11:18, 21, 32; 13:40; in later editions, see also 1 Ne. 19:10, 13; 2 Ne. 10:3–4; 11:7; 25:12; 26:12; 30:2; Mos. 3:5, 8; 5:15; 7:27; 13:28, 33, 34; 15:1–5; 16:15; Al. 11:28–32, 35, 38, 39, 44; 42:15; He. 9:22–23; 14:12; 3 Ne. 1:14; 5:20; 11:14; 15:5; 19:18; Morm. 3:21; 9:11–12; Eth. 3:14; 4:7, 12; Moses 1:16–17; D&C 84:19–25.

10. Joseph Smith, Jr., *History of The Church of Jesus Christ of Latter-day Saints*, ed. B. H. Roberts, 2d ed. rev., 7 vols. (Salt Lake City: Deseret News, 1932–51), 5:94, 127; D&C 109.

11. See Andrew F. Ehat and Lyndon W. Cook, comps. and eds., *The Words of Joseph Smith: The Contemporary Accounts of the Nauvoo Discourses of the Prophet Joseph* (Provo, UT: Brigham Young University Religious Studies Center, 1980), 198, 221, 229, 356.

12. *Times and Seasons* 3 (15 Nov. 1841): 578.

13. Stan Larson, "The King Follett Discourse: A Newly Amalgamated Text," *Brigham Young University Studies* 18 (Winter 1978): 198–208.

14. See, for example, 2 Ne. 9:5; Mos. 3:8; 4:2; 7:27; 26:23; Al. 5:15; He. 14:12; 3 Ne. 9:15; Eth. 3:15–16; 4:7; D&C 14:9; 38:1–3; 45:1; 76:23–24; 88:7–10; 93:8–10; Moses 1:32–33; 2:1.

15. See G. Homer Durham, ed., "Discourse by President Brigham Young Delivered in the Bowery, Great Salt Lake City, August 4, 1867," *Utah Historical Quarterly* 29 (1961): 68–69; Brigham Young, et al., *Journal of Discourses*, 26 vols. (Liverpool: Latter-day Saints' Book Depot, 1855–86), 1:238; 2:30; 8:228; 9:240, 286; 11:327; 12:99; 13:236; 14:41 (hereafter JD, followed by volume and pages numbers).

16. JD 9:286.

17. Ibid., 12:99.

18. See David John Buerger, "The Adam-God Doctrine," *Dialogue: A Journal of Mormon Thought* 15 (Spring 1982): 14–58.

19. Brigham Young, unpublished discourse, 19 Feb. 1954, archives, Historical Department, Church of Jesus Christ of Latter-day Saints, Salt Lake City; hereafter church archives.

20. On resurrected beings, see JD 4:133, 217; 6:275; 8:341; 15:137; 17:143; on Jesus as creator, see JD 1:270; 3:80–81; 7:3, 163; 11:279; on Elohim as grandfather, see JD 4:215–19; 9:148; 13:311; Brigham Young, unpublished discourse, 5 Feb. 1852, church archives.

21. Brigham Young, unpublished discourse, 25 April 1855, church archives; JD 9:286, 327.

22. In Culley K. Christensen, *The Adam-God Maze* (Scottsdale, AZ: Independent Publishers, 1981), 274–75.

23. See JD 2:6.

24. Salt Lake School of the Prophets Minute Book, 9 June 1873, church archives. Young felt that even the Book of Mormon would have been translated differently if done in his day, given the progress the Saints had made in understanding (JD 9:311).

25. John Taylor, *The Mediation and Atonement* (Salt Lake City: Deseret News, 1882), 150–51; also pp. 94, 123, 127, 138, 166, 192, and JD 1:153–54, 223, 369–70; 10:50, 55; 11:22; 14:247–48; 15:217; 24:34, 125, 227; 25:305.

26. *Sacred Hymns and Spiritual Songs for The Church of Jesus Christ of Latter-day Saints* (Salt Lake City: Deseret News, 1891), 295, no. 262.

27. *Latter-day Saints' Millennial Star* 11 (15 Sept. 1849): 281–84; (15 Oct. 1849): 309–12.

28. *Juvenile Instructor* 6 (30 Sept. 1871): 155.

29. Franklin D. Richards and James A. Little, *A Compendium of the Faith and Doctrine of The Church of Jesus Christ of Latter-day Saints* (Salt Lake City: Deseret News, 1882), 78–79.

30. Taylor, *Mediation and Atonement*, 138.

31. JD 26:300.

32. Ibid., 26:172.

33. See Buerger, 20, 31, 33–34, 37–38, 52n74.

34. Abraham H. Cannon Journal, 23 June 1889, photocopy at church archives.

35. *Deseret News Weekly* 47 (7 Oct. 1893): 506; *Latter-day Saints' Millennial Star* 57 (24 Jan. 1895): 52, 65; *Juvenile Instructor* 35 (1 Feb. 1900): 90–91.

36. Christensen, 206–37; Buerger, 32–34, 53n76; St. George Stake High Council Minutes, 13 Dec. 1890, church archives.

37. St. George Stake High Council Minutes, 13 Dec. 1890; see also the letter of Edward Bunker, Sr., recorded in these minutes, 15 May 1891, and also in the Edward Bunker Autobiography, 32–49, church archives; and Joseph F. Smith to Bishop Bunker, 27 Feb. 1902, Joseph F. Smith Letterbooks, church archives.

38. St. George Stake High Council Minutes, 11 June 1892.

39. James R. Clark, comp., *Messages of the First Presidency of The Church of Jesus Christ of Latter-day Saints*, 6 vols. (Salt Lake City: Bookcraft, 1965–75), 3:243.

40. *Latter-day Saints' Millennial Star* 57 (6 June 1895): 355–56.

41. Edward Stevenson Diary, 3 March and 28 Feb. 1896, church archives.

42. See Buerger, 36–42.

43. Ibid., 38–43.

44. Ibid., 31, 47n19, 52ns61, 63, 65, 68.

45. Ibid., 41–42.

46. *Improvement Era* 15 (April 1912): 483–85; *Juvenile Instructor* 50 (Oct. 1915): 649.

47. Clark, 4:267.

48. James E. Talmage, *Jesus the Christ* (Salt Lake City: Deseret News, 1915), 32–41.

49. See *Juvenile Instructor* 50 (Oct. 1915): 649; *Improvement Era* 18 (Sept. 1915): 1,011.

50. See Buerger, 43–44.

51. *Conference Reports*, 6 April 1916, 15–19.

52. Anthon H. Lund Diary, 29 June 1916, church archives; George F. Richards Diary, 29 June 1916, church archives; *Improvement Era* 19 (Aug. 1916): 934–42.

53. For a much fuller treatment of Elohim and Jehovah in the scriptures, see my "Elohim and Jehovah in Mormonism and the Bible," *Dialogue: A Journal of Mormon Thought* 19 (Spring 1986), 1: 77–93.

54. See Bruce R. McConkie, *The Promised Messiah* (Salt Lake City: Deseret Book, 1978), 101–102; *The Mortal Messiah, Book 3* (Salt Lake City: Deseret Book, 1980), 386; see also *The Old Testament Part Two, Gospel Doctrine Teachers' Supplement* (Salt Lake City: The Church of Jesus Christ of Latter-day Saints, 1980), 110.

55. See McConkie, *The Promised Messiah*, 335–37, 561–62.

56. See McConkie, "Our Relationship with the Lord," BYU Devotional Address, 2 March 1982, 5, 19–20, typescript in my possession.

57. Lowell L. Bennion, "The Mormon Christianizing of the Old Testament: A Response," *Sunstone* 5 (Nov./Dec. 1980): 40.

58. See, for example, *Old Testament, Part Two*, 102–11.

59. See McConkie, *The Promised Messiah*, 107–10; Mark E. Petersen, *Christ, Jehovah and the Witnesses* (pamphlet for reference use by missionaries, n.d.), 2–10.

60. "Christ as the Father," Lesson 16 in the *1979–1980 Melchezidek Priesthood Personal Study Guide* (Salt Lake City: The Church of Jesus Christ of Latter-day Saints, 1979), 92–97.

61. Compare B. H. Roberts's two works, *Rasha—The Jew* (Salt Lake City: Deseret News Press, 1932), and the earlier *The Mormon Doctrine of Deity* (1903; reprint ed., Salt Lake City: Horizon Publishers, n.d.).

62. See Roberts, *Rasha*, 28–29, 32–34; Joseph Fielding Smith, *Answers to Gospel Questions*, 5 vols. (Salt Lake City: Deseret Book, 1979), 1:13–21; Talmage, 32–41.

63. See Eugene Seaich, *Ancient Texts and Mormonism* (Sandy, UT: Mormon Miscellaneous, 1983), 12–28.

5.
The Reconstruction of Mormon Doctrine

Thomas G. Alexander

ONE OF THE BARRIERS TO UNDERSTANDING MORMON THEOLOGY is the underlying assumption by most Latter-day Saints that doctrine develops consistently, that ideas build cumulatively on each other. As a result, older revelations are usually interpreted by referring to current doctrinal positions. This type of interpretation may produce systematic theology and may satisfy those trying to understand and internalize current doctrine, but it is bad history since it leaves an unwarranted impression of continuity and consistency.

By examining particular beliefs at specific junctures in Mormon history, I hope to explore how certain key Mormon doctrines have developed over time. I have made every effort to restate each doctrine as contemporaries most likely understood it, without superimposing later developments. I focus on the period 1830–35, the initial era of Mormon doctrinal development, and on the period 1893–1925, when much of contemporary doctrine seems to have been systematized. Since a full exposition of all doctrines is impossible in a short essay, I have singled out the doctrines of God and man.[1]

The Book of Mormon tended to define God as an absolute personage of spirit who, clothed in flesh, revealed himself in Jesus Christ (see Abinadi's sermon to King Noah in Mos. 13–14). Two years later, the first issue of the Mormon *Evening and Morning Star* published a similar description of God in the "Articles and Covenants of the Church of Christ," the church's first statement of faith and practice which, with some additions, became Doctrine and Covenants 20.

53

The "Articles," according to correspondence in the *Star*, was used with the Book of Mormon in proselytizing and indicated that "there is a God in heaven who is infinite and eternal, from everlasting to everlasting, the same unchangeable God, the framer of heaven and earth and all things which are in them." The *Messenger and Advocate*, successor to the *Star*, published lectures 5 and 6 of the "Lectures on Faith" of the Doctrine and Covenants (1835), defining the "Father" as "the only supreme governor, and independent being, in whom all fulness and perfection dwells; who is omnipotent, omnipresent, and omniscient; without beginning of days or end of life." In a letter published in the *Messenger and Advocate*, Warren A. Cowdery argued that "we have proven to the satisfaction of every intelligent being, that there is a great first cause, prime mover, self-existent, independent and all wise being whom we call God . . . immutable in his purposes and unchangable in his nature."[2]

These early works did not address the question of *ex nihilo* creation, and there is little evidence that early church doctrine specifically differentiated between Christ and God.[3] Indeed, this distinction was probably considered unnecessary since the early discussion also seems to have supported trinitarian doctrine. Joseph Smith's 1832 account of his first vision spoke only of one personage and did not make the explicit separation of God and Christ found in the 1838 version. The Book of Mormon declared that Mary "is the mother of God, after the manner of the flesh," which was changed in 1837 to "mother of the Son of God." Abinadi's sermon in the Book of Mormon explored the relationship between God and Christ: "God himself shall come down among the children of men, and shall redeem his people. And because he dwelleth in the flesh he shall be called the Son of God, and having subjected the flesh to the will of the Father, being the Father and the Son—The Father, because he was conceived by the power of God; and the Son, because of the flesh; thus becoming the Father and Son—And they are one God, yea, the very Eternal Father of heaven and of earth" (Mos. 15:1–4).[4]

The "Lectures on Faith" differentiated between the Father and Son more explicitly, but even they did not define a materialistic, tritheistic godhead. In announcing the publication of the Doctrine and Covenants, which included the lectures, the *Messenger and Advocate* commented that it trusted the volume would give "the churches abroad . . . a perfect understanding of the doctrine believed by this society." The lectures declared that "there are two personages who constitute the great matchless, governing and supreme power over all things—by whom all things were created and made." They are "the Father being a personage of spirit" and "the Son, who was in the bosom of the Father, a personage of tabernacle, made, or fashioned like unto man, or being in the form and likeness of man, or, rather, man was formed after his likeness, and in his image." The "Articles and Covenants" called the Father, Son, and Holy Ghost "one God" rather than "Godhead," a term Mormons use today to separate themselves from trinitarians.[5]

The doctrine of the Holy Ghost in these early sources is even more striking compared to our point of view today. The "Lectures on Faith" defined the Holy Ghost as the mind of the Father and the Son, a member of the Godhead but not a personage, who binds the Father and Son together (D&C, 1835 ed., 53–54). This view of the Holy Ghost likely reinforced trinitarian doctrine by explaining how personal beings like the Father and Son become one god through the noncorporeal presence of a shared mind.

If the doctrines of the Godhead in the early church were close to trinitarian doctrine, the teachings of man seemed quite close to Methodist Arminianism, which saw humanity as creatures of God but capable of sanctification. Alma's commandments to Corianton (Al. 39–42) defined man as a creation of God who became "carnal, sensual, and devilish by nature" after the Fall (Al. 42:10). Man was in the hand of justice, and mercy from God was impossible without the atonement of Christ. King Benjamin's discussion of creation, Adam's fall, and the Atonement (Mos. 2–4) viewed man and all creation as creatures of God (Mos. 2:23–26; 4:9, 19, 21). Warren Cowdery's letter in the *Messenger and Advocate* argued that although "man is the more noble and intelligent part of this lower creation, to whom the other grades in the scale of being are subject, yet, the man is dependent on the great first cause and is constantly upheld by him, therefore justly amenable to him."[6]

The Book of Mormon included a form of the doctrine of original sin, in which everyone is sinful simply because of his or her humanity. Although sinfulness inhered in humankind from the fall of Adam according to early works, it applied to individual men and women only from the age of accountability and ability to repent, not from birth. Very young children were free from this sin, but every accountable person merited punishment. Lehi's discussion of the necessity of opposition in all things (2 Ne. 2: 7–13) made such sinfulness a necessary part of God's plan, since the law, the Atonement, and righteousness—indeed the fulfillment of the purposes of creation—were contingent upon humanity's sinfulness. An article in the *Evening and Morning Star* attributed this "seed of corruption" to the "depravity of nature" which "can never be entirely effaced": "Because we were born in sin, the Gospel concludes that we ought to apply all our attentive endeavors to eradicate the seeds of corruption. And, because the image of the Creator is partly erased from our hearts, the Gospel concludes that we ought to give ourselves wholly to the retracing of it, and so to answer the excellence of our extraction."[7]

These early church works also exhibit a form of Christian perfectionism, which held people capable of freely choosing to become perfect like God and Christ but which rejected irresistible grace. The *Evening and Morning Star* said that "God has created man with a mind capable of instruction, and a faculty which may be enlarged in proportion to the heed and diligence given to the light communicated from heaven to the intellect; and that the nearer man approaches perfection, the more conspicuous are his views, and the greater his enjoyments, until he has overcome the evils of this life and lost every desire of sin; and like the ancients, arrives to that point of faith that he is wrapped in the power and glory of his Maker and is caught up to dwell with him." The "Lectures on Faith" argued that we can become perfect if we purify ourselves to become "holy as he is holy, and perfect as he is perfect," and thus like Christ.[8] A similar sentiment was expressed in the Book of Mormon, in Moroni 10:32, which declared "that by his grace ye may be perfect in Christ."

On the doctrines of God and humanity, the position of the LDS church between 1830 and 1835 was probably closest to that of the Disciples of Christ and the Methodists, although differences existed. Alexander Campbell, for instance, objected to the term "Trinity" but argued that "the Father is of none, neither begotten nor proceding; the Son is eternally begotten of the Father; the Holy Ghost eternally proceeding from the Father and the Son." Methodist teaching was more explicitly trinitarian than that of either the Disciples or the Mormons. All three groups believed in an absolute spiritual father. Methodists, Disciples, and Mormons also believed to some degree in the perfectibility of man. As Alexander Campbell put it, "Perfection is . . . the glory and felicity of man. . . . There is a true, a real perfectibility of human character and of human nature, through the soul-redeeming mediation and holy spiritual influence of the great Philanthropist." Methodists believed that all "real Christians are so perfect as not to live in outward sin."[9]

Mormons rejected Calvinistic doctrines of election, which were basically at odds with their belief in perfectionism and free will, but so did the Methodists and Disciples. In discussing the Fall and redemption, Book of Mormon prophet Nephi declared that "Adam fell that men might be and men are that they might have joy" (2 Ne. 2:25). This joy was found through the redemption from the Fall which allowed men to "act for themselves and not to be acted upon, save it be by the punishment of the law at the great and last day, according to the commandments which God hath given" (2 Ne. 2:26). Like Methodist doctrine, however, the LDS doctrine of perfectionism began with the sovereignty of God and the depravity of unregenerate man. But a careful reading of Mormon scriptures and doctrinal statements reveals that LDS doctrine went beyond the beliefs of the Disciples and Methodists in differentiating more clearly between Father and Son and in anticipating the possibility of human perfection through the atonement of Jesus Christ.[10]

Nevertheless, that there was disagreement—often violent—between the Mormons and other denominations is evident. The careful student of the Latter-day Saint past needs to determine, however, where the source of disagreement lay. Campbell, in his *Delusions, An Analysis of the Book of Mormon*, lumped Joseph Smith with other false Christs because of his claims to authority and revelation from God, and he objected to some doctrines. He also attacked the sweeping and authoritative nature of the Book of Mormon with the comment that Smith "decides all the great controversies—infant baptism, ordination, the trinity, regeneration, repentance, justification, eternal punishment, [and] who may baptize." But he also recognized, somewhat backhandedly, that the Book of Mormon spoke to contemporary Christians: "The Nephites, like their fathers for many generations, were good Christians, believers in the doctrines of the Calvinists and Methodists." Campbell and others before 1835 objected principally to claims of authority, modern revelation, miracles, and communitarianism, not to the doctrines of God and man.[11]

During the remaining years of Joseph Smith's life and into
the late nineteenth century, various doctrines were proposed, some
of which were abandoned and others adopted in the reconstruction
of Mormon doctrine after 1890. Joseph Smith and other church
leaders laid the basis for the reconstruction with revelation and
doctrinal exposition between 1832 and 1844. Three influences seem
to have been responsible for the questions leading to these revelations and insights. First was the work of Joseph Smith and others,
particularly Sidney Rigdon, on the inspired revision of the Bible
(especially John's Gospel and some of the letters of John). Questions
which arose in the course of revision led to the revelations in Doctrine and Covenants 76 and 93, and perhaps section 88. These revelations were particularly important because they carried the doctrine of perfectionism far beyond anything generally acceptable to
contemporary Protestants, including Methodists. Evidence from the
period indicates, however, that the implications of this doctrine were
not generally evident in the Mormon community until 1838.

The second influence was the persecution of the Saints in
Jackson County, Missouri. This persecution also intensified the emphasis on perfectionism — which eventually led to the doctrine of
eternal progression. As the Saints suffered and persevered, the
Evening and Morning Star reemphasized the idea that the faithful
could become Christlike, and a side of man's nature quite apart from
his fallen state was thus affirmed.[12]

The third influence was the work of Joseph Smith and others
on the "Book of Abraham." Although Joseph Smith and others seem
to have worked on the first two chapters of this book following 1835,
the parts following chapter 2 dealing with a plurality of gods were
not written until 1842. Still Doctrine and Covenants 121:31–32 indicate that Joseph Smith believed in a plurality of gods as early as
1839.[13]

Thereafter, between 1842 and 1844, Joseph Smith spoke on
and published radical Christian doctrines such as the plurality of
gods, the tangibility of God's body, the distinct separation of God
and Christ, the potential of man to become and function as a god,
the explicit rejection of *ex nihilo* creation, and the materiality of
everything, including spirit. These ideas were perhaps most clearly
stated in the King Follett discourse of April 1844.[14]

It seems clear that certain ideas which developed between

1832 and 1844 were internalized after 1835 and accepted by the Latter-day Saints. This was particularly true of the material anthropomorphism of God and Jesus Christ, advanced perfectionism as elaborated in the doctrine of eternal progression, and the potential godhood of humanity.

Between 1845 and 1890, however, certain doctrines were proposed which were later rejected or modified. In an address to the rulers of the world in 1845, for instance, the Council of the Twelve Apostles wrote of the "great Eloheem Jehovah" as though the two names were synonymous, indicating that the identification of Jehovah and Christ had little meaning to contemporaries. In addition, Brigham Young preached that Adam was not only the first man but also the god of this world. Acceptance of the King Follett doctrine would have granted the possibility of Adam being a god, but the idea that he was the god of this world conflicted with the later Jehovah-Christ doctrine. Doctrines such as those preached by Orson Pratt, harking back to the "Lectures on Faith" and emphasizing the absolute nature of God, and Amasa Lyman, stressing radical perfectionism which denied the necessity of Christ's atonement, were variously questioned by the First Presidency and twelve apostles. In Lyman's case, his beliefs contributed to his excommunication.[15]

The newer and older doctrines thus coexisted, and all competed with novel positions spelled out by various church leaders. The "Lectures on Faith" continued to appear as part of the Doctrine and Covenants in a section entitled "Doctrine and Covenants"— distinguished from the "Covenants and Commandments," which constitute the current LDS Doctrine and Covenants. The Pearl of Great Price containing the "Book of Abraham" was published in England in 1851 as a missionary tract and was accepted as authoritative in 1880. The earliest versions of Apostle Parley P. Pratt's *Key to the Science of Theology* and Brigham H. Roberts's *The Gospel: An Exposition of Its First Principles* both emphasized an omnipresent, non-personal Holy Ghost, although Pratt's emphasis was radically materialistic and Roberts's more allegorical. Both were elaborating ideas addressed in the King Follett sermon. Such fluidity of doctrine, unusual from a twentieth-century perspective, characterized the nineteenth-century church.

By 1890 the doctrines preached in the church combined what would seem today both familiar and strange. Yet between 1890 and 1925 these doctrine were reconstructed principally on the basis of works by four European immigrants, James E. Talmage, Brigham H. Roberts, John A. Widtsoe, and Charles W. Penrose. Widtsoe, Penrose, and Talmage did much of their writing before they became apostles, but Roberts served as a member of the First Council of the Seventy during the entire period.

Perhaps the most important doctrine addressed was the doctrine of the Godhead, which was reconstructed beginning in 1893 and 1894. During that year Talmage, president of Latter-day Saints University in Salt Lake City and later president and professor of geology at the University of Utah, gave a series of lectures on the "Articles of Faith" to the theological class of LDSU. In the fall of 1898 the First Presidency asked him to rewrite the lectures and present them for approval as an exposition of church doctrines. In the process, Talmage reconsidered and reconstructed the doctrine of the Holy Ghost. In response to questions raised by Talmage's lectures, George Q. Cannon, of the First Presidency, "commenting on the ambiguity existing in our printed works concerning the nature or character of the Holy Ghost, expressed his opinion that the Holy Ghost was in reality a person, in the image of the other members of the Godhead—a man in form and figure; and that what we often speak of as the Holy Ghost is in reality but the power or influence of the spirit." The First Presidency on that occasion, however, "deemed it wise to say as little as possible on this as on other disputed subjects."[16]

In 1894 Talmage published an article in the *Juvenile Instructor* elaborating on his and Cannon's views. He incorporated the article almost verbatim into his manuscript for the *Articles of Faith*, and the presidency approved the article virtually without change in 1898.

The impact of the *Articles of Faith* on doctrinal exposition within the church was enormous. Some doctrinal works, including B. H. Roberts's 1888 volume *The Gospel*, were quite allegorical on the nature of God, Christ, and the Holy Ghost. In the 1901 edition, after the publication of the *Articles of Faith*, Roberts explicitly revised his view of the Godhead, modifying his discussion and incorporating Talmage's more literal interpretation of the Holy Ghost.

By 1900 it was impossible to consider the doctrines of God and humanity without dealing with organic evolution. Charles

Darwin's *Origin of Species* had been in print for four decades, and scientific advances together with changing attitudes had introduced many secular-rational ideas. Talmage and John A. Widtsoe had confronted these ideas as they studied at universities in the United States and elsewhere. In a February 1900 article, for example, Talmage argued that science and religion had to be reconciled since "faith is not blind submission, passive obedience, with no effort at thought or reason. Faith, if worthy of its name, rests upon truth; and truth is the foundation of science."[17]

Just as explicit in his approach was Widtsoe, who came to the conclusion that the "scriptural proof of the truth of the gospel had been quite fully developed and was unanswerable." He "set out therefore to present [his] modest contributions from the point of view of science and those trained in that type of thinking." Between November 1903 and July 1904, he published a series of articles in the *Improvement Era* under the title "Joseph Smith as Scientist." The articles, republished in 1908 as the Young Men's Mutual Improvement Association course of study, argued that Joseph Smith anticipated many scientific theories and discoveries.[18]

Joseph Smith as Scientist, like Widtsoe's later *A Rational Theology*, drew heavily on Herbert Spencer's theories and ideas. The Mormon gospel, Widtsoe argued, recognized the reality of time, space, and matter. The universe is both material and eternal, and God organized rather than created it. Thus God was not the creator, nor was he omnipotent. He too was governed by natural law, which was fundamental.

Although the publications of Talmage, Roberts, and Widtsoe established the church's basic doctrines of the Godhead, some members and non-members were still confused. In 1911 Apostle George F. Richards spoke in the tabernacle on the nature of God. Afterward a member challenged him, arguing that Father, Son, and Holy Ghost were one God rather than three distinct beings. Richards disagreed and cited scriptural references, including Joseph Smith's first vision.[19]

In February 1912 detractors confronted missionaries in the Central States Mission with the Adam-God theory. In a letter to the mission president, the First Presidency argued that Brigham Young did not mean to say that Adam was God, and at a special priesthood meeting during the April 1912 General Conference, they secured approval for a declaration that Mormons worship God the Father, not Adam.[20]

Reconsideration of the doctrine of God and the ambiguity in discourse and printed works over the relationship between God the Father and Jesus Christ pointed to the need for an authoritative statement on the nature and mission of Christ.

From 1904 to 1906 Talmage delivered a series of lectures on "Jesus the Christ" at Latter-day Saints University. The First Presidency again asked Talmage to incorporate the lectures into a book, but he suspended the work to fill other assignments. In September 1914, however, the presidency asked him to prepare "the book with as little delay as possible." In order to free him "from visits and telephone calls" and "in view of the importance of the work," Talmage was "directed to occupy a room in the Temple where" he would "be free from interruption." After completing the writing in April 1915, he said that he had "felt the inspiration of the place and . . . appreciated the privacy and quietness incident thereto." The presidency and twelve raised some questions about specific portions, but they agreed generally with the work, which elaborated views expressed previously in the *Articles of Faith*.[21]

By 1916 the ideas which Joseph Smith and other leaders had proposed (generally after 1835) were serving as the framework for continued development of the doctrine of God. Talmage, Widtsoe, and Roberts had undertaken a reconstruction which carried doctrine far beyond anything described in the "Lectures on Faith" or generally believed by church members prior to 1835.

Official statements were soon required to canonize doctrines on the Father and the Son, particularly because of the ambiguity in the scriptures and in authoritative statements about the unity of the Father and the Son, the role of Jesus Christ as Father, and the roles of the Father and Son in the Creation. A statement for the church membership prepared by the First Presidency and twelve apostles, apparently first drafted by Talmage, was published in 1916. The statement made clear the separate corporeal nature of the two beings and delineated their roles in the creation of the earth and their continued relationships with this creation. The statement was congruent with the King Follett discourse and the work of Talmage, Widtsoe, and Roberts.[22]

This elaboration, together with the revised doctrine of the

Holy Ghost, made necessary the revision and redefinition of works previously used. By January 1915, Charles W. Penrose had completed a revision of Parley P. Pratt's *Key to the Science of Theology*. Penrose deleted or altered passages which discussed the Holy Ghost as non-personal and which posited a sort of "spiritual fluid" pervading the universe.[23]

Less than two years later, in November 1917, a meeting of the twelve apostles and First Presidency considered the question of the "Lectures on Faith," particularly lecture 5. At that time, they agreed to append a footnote in the next edition, apparently clarifying the lecture's teachings on God. This proved unnecessary when the First Presidency appointed a committee to revise the entire Doctrine and Covenants.[24]

Revision continued through July and August 1921, and the church printed the new edition in late 1921. The committee proposed to delete the "Lectures on Faith" on the ground that they were "lessons prepared for use in the School of the Elders, conducted in Kirtland, Ohio, during the winter of 1834–35; but they were never presented to nor accepted by the Church as being otherwise than theological lectures or lessons." How the committee came to this conclusion is uncertain. The General Conference of the church in April 1835 had accepted the entire volume, including the lectures, as authoritative and binding upon church members. What seems certain, however, is that the 1916 official statement, based upon Talmage's, Widtsoe's, and Roberts's reconstructed doctrine of the Godhead, had superceded the theology of the lectures.

Talmage, Widtsoe, and Roberts devoted at least as much effort to considering the doctrine of man as they did the doctrine of God, but their work did not lead to the kind of authoritative statement on man which was issued by the First Presidency on God. For example, Talmage argued for a radical doctrine of free will, which essentially rejected the ideas implicit in the Book of Mormon by denying man's predisposition under any conditions to evil, whether before or after the Fall, and defended the possibility of progressing among the three degrees of glory. Roberts espoused a materialistic theology of man and God, including the importance of sexual relationships, here and hereafter, for procreation and love, and also advocated the eternal existence of individuals as conscious, self-existing entities or intelligences. Widtsoe too endorsed the eternal nature of human consciousness and even suggested that there was a time when there was no God. Not all church leaders, however, favored these progressive ideas.[25]

Several possible reasons for the failure to settle questions regarding man seem plausible. First, it may be that the church leaders and members generally considered such questions settled by doctrines implicit in the Book of Mormon and other teachings of the period before 1835. Second, it may be that they generally took for granted the doctrines of the King Follett discourse and the progressive theologians. Or third, it may be that the church membership never thoroughly considered the implications of the problems.

Given the available sources, it seems probable that the reason questions were not authoritatively resolved is a combination of the second and third hypotheses. Basically, concern over the increasing vigor of the theory of evolution through natural selection seems to have outweighed all other considerations on the doctrine of man. The First Presidency wanted to see the truths of science and religion reconciled, and much of the work of Talmage, Widtsoe, and Roberts dealt with that challenge. On evolution, for instance, they generally took the view that while evolution itself was a correct principle, the idea of natural selection was not. The First Presidency's official statements of 1909 and 1925 specifically addressed the problem of evolution and of human nature, which was an important part of Talmage's, Widtsoe's, and Roberts's works.[26]

Because evolution was constantly in the background, it seems apparent that two things happened. First, church members internalized the implications of the doctrine of eternal progression, assuming that men and women, as gods in embryo, were basically godlike and that the flesh itself, since it was common to both God and humanity, posed no barrier to human perfectibility. Second, members seem to have concluded that Joseph Smith's statement in the "Articles of Faith" that God would not punish man for Adam's transgression was a rejection of the doctrine of original sin, which held that humanity inherited a condition of sinfulness. In general, it seemed, the doctrine of absolute free will demanded that any evil which man might do resulted not from the flesh but from a conscious choice. How these, and related doctrines, will change in the future remains to be seen.

– NOTES –

1. Readers interested in a fuller treatment should see my "The Reconstruction of Mormon Doctrine: From Joseph Smith to Progressive Theology," *Sunstone* 5 (July/Aug. 1980), 4:24–33.

2. *Evening and Morning Star* (Kirtland, OH, reprint edition), June 1832, 2; May 1833, 189; W. A. Cowdery to Editor, 17 March 1835, *Messenger and Advocate*, May 1835, 113.

3. Al. 18:28; 22:9–12; 1 Ne. 17:36; D&C 14:9; 45:1; James R. Clark, *Messages of the First Presidency of the Church of Jesus Christ of Latter-day Saints, 1833-1964*, 6 vols. (Salt Lake City: Bookcraft, 1965–75), 1:27.

4. Milton V. Backman, Jr., *Joseph Smith's First Vision: The First Vision in Its Historical Context* (Salt Lake City: Bookcraft, 1971), 155–57; Richard P. Howard, *Restoration Scriptures: A Study of Their Textual Development* (Independence, MO: Herald House, 1969), 47–48; James B. Allen, "Line Upon Line," *Ensign*, July 1979, 37–38.

5. *Messenger and Advocate*, May 1835, 122–23; D&C 20:28.

6. *Messenger and Advocate*, May 1835, 113.

7. *Evening and Morning Star*, Oct. 1832, 77.

8. Ibid., March 1834, 283; D&C 1835 ed., 67.

9. Alexander Campbell, *A Compendium of Alexander Campbell's Theology*, ed. Royal Humbert (St. Louis, MO: Bethany Press, 1961), 85, 231; Jonathan Crowther, *A True and Complete Portraiture of Methodism* (New York: Daniel Hitt and Thomas Ware, 1813), 143, 178.

10. Sydney E. Ahlstrom, *A Religious History of the American People*, 2 vols. (New York: Doubleday, 1975), 1:532.

11. Alexander Campbell, *Delusions, An Analysis of the Book of Mormon With an Examination of Its Internal and External Evidences, and a Refutation of Its Pretences to Divine Authority With Prefatory Remarks by Joshua V. Himes* (Boston: Benjamin H. Greene, 1832), 5–7, 12–14. See also *Evangelical Enquirer* (Dayton, OH), 7 March 1831, 1:235–26; *Evangelical Magazine and Gospel Advocate* (New Series, 1913), 2:47; *Niles Weekly Register*, 16 July 1831, 353; and *The Encyclopedia of Religious Knowledge* (Brattleboro: Fessenden & Co., 1835), 844.

12. See *Evening and Morning Star*, Jan. 1834, 256; March 1834, 283.

13. James B. Allen and Glen M. Leonard, *The Story of the Latter-day Saints* (Salt Lake City: Deseret Book, 1976), 67–68.

14. See T. Edgar Lyon, "Doctrinal Development of the Church During the Nauvoo Sojourn, 1839–1846," *Brigham Young University Studies* 15 (Summer 1975): 435–66; Stan Larson, "The King Follett Discourse: A Newly Amalgamated Text," *Brigham Young University Studies* 18 (Winter 1978): 193–208; Van Hale, "The Doctrinal Impact of the King Follett Discourse," ibid., 209–25.

15. Clark, *Messages*, 1:253; 2:233–40; Brigham Young et al., *Journal of*

Discourses, 26 vols. (Liverpool: Latter-day Saints' Book Depot, 1855–86), 1:50–51; 7:299–302; Ronald W. Walker, "The Godbeite Protest in the Making of Modern Utah," Ph.D. diss., University of Utah, 1977, 183.

16. James E. Talmage Journal, 5 Jan. 1899, Special Collections, Harold B. Lee Library, Brigham Young University, Provo, Utah; *Juvenile Instructor* 29 (1 April 1894): 220; James E. Talmage, *The Articles of Faith: A Series of Lectures on the Principal Doctrines of the Church of Jesus Christ of Latter-day Saints* (Salt Lake City: Deseret News, 1899), 164–65. See also Ken Cannon, "The Development of the Mormon Understanding of the Nature of the Holy Ghost," *Seventh East Press*, 12 April 1982, 9–10.

17. *Improvement Era*, Feb. 1900, 256.

18. John A. Widtsoe, *In a Sunlit Land: The Autobiography of John A. Widtsoe* (Salt Lake City: Milton R. Hunter and G. Homer Durham, 1952), 66–67; *Joseph Smith as Scientist: A Contribution to Mormon Philosophy* (Salt Lake City: YMMIA General Board, 1908).

19. George F. Richards Journal, 28 March 1911, archives, Historical Department, Church of Jesus Christ of Latter-day Saints, Salt Lake City; hereafter church archives.

20. Clark, *Messages*, 4:266; Anthon H. Lund Journal, 8 April 1912, church archives.

21. Talmage Journal, 14 Sept. 1914, 19 April 1915; Lund Journal, 4, 6 May 1915; Richards Journal, 15, 24 June 1915; Heber J. Grant Journal, 18, 20 May, 8, 10 June 1915, church archives; Clark, *Messages*, 4:399–400; James E. Talmage, *Jesus the Christ* (Salt Lake City: Deseret News, 1915).

22. Clark, *Messages*, 5:23–24.

23. Lund Journal, 21 Jan. 1915.

24. Grant Journal, 15 Nov. 1917, 20 Aug. 1920; Talmage Journal, 3 Jan. 1918, 11 March 1921; Richards Journal, 11 March, 29 July 1921. The principal reason for the committee was the worn condition of the printer's plates and the discrepancies existing between the current edition and Roberts's edition of Joseph Smith's *History of the Church*.

25. This is discussed at greater length in my *Sunstone* essay, "The Reconstruction of Mormon Doctrine," 30–31.

26. See Clark, *Messages*, 4:199–206; 5:243–44.

6.
Omnipotence, Omnipresence, and Omniscience in Mormon Theology

Kent E. Robson

HISTORICALLY, MORMON THEOLOGY HAS DIFFERED FROM TRADI-
tional Christianity in many ways: ascribing to God a tabernacle of
flesh and bones, teaching a plurality of gods, denying an *ex nihilo*
creation, asserting that individuals and nature have necessary being,
promoting the idea that God became God through a process of
progression, and claiming that all nature (including spirit) is material. Given such differences, it is not surprising that most Mormons—at least until recently—have tended not to use terms such as
omniscience (all-knowing), omnipotence (all-powerful), and omni-
presence (all-present) to refer to God.

But Mormon scriptures themselves say that "God knoweth
all things."[1] The second lecture of the "Lectures on Faith" (which
appeared in all editions of the Doctrine and Covenants until 1921),
regardless of its authorship, stated explicitly that God is omniscient.[2] And the official LDS publication, *Gospel Principles*, reiterated
this for Mormons in 1978.[3] Certainly such assurances are sufficient
for religious faith, but if one hopes to acquire a deeper understanding of God and his ways, he or she must ask if God's knowledge,
power, or presence is absolutely unlimited—if God is in time or
outside of time.

There are many different ideas of omniscience and omnipotence, and it is important in Mormon theology to decide which
concept we have adopted and which we ought to adopt. The scriptures are not self-interpreting and must be approached cautiously
and sensitively, for they were given in human language, to prophets
who themselves have preconceptions and who may not have previously understood the idea being expressed in the revelation (see
D&C 1:24).

Even in traditional Christianity God's omniscience and
omnipotence have rarely been assumed to be total and unlimited. St.
Thomas Aquinas represents the theology that Mormon philosopher
Sterling McMurrin describes as "the absolutistic tradition" (in contrast to Mormonism's "finitist tradition").[4] Still, Aquinas did not
believe in the total omniscience or omnipotence of God. For example, God cannot know or do (or be required to know or do) things
that are not true, that cannot be done, or that are self-contradictory.
Rather, God knows or does only those things which "in any way
are"[5] — that is, only those things which can be known or done.

This same point was made by LDS church leader B. H.
Roberts, perhaps the most perceptive of "official" Mormon theologians, when he wrote in the fourth-year manual of *The Seventy's Course
in Theology* that "the ascription of the attribute of Omnipotence to
God" is affected by what "may or can be done by power conditioned
by other external existences — duration, space, matter, truth, justice.... So with the All-knowing attribute Omniscience," Roberts
continued, "that must be understood somewhat in the same light . . .
not that God is Omniscient up to the point that further progress in
knowledge is impossible to him; but that all knowledge that is, all
that exists, God knows."[6]

We do not limit, in my opinion, the concept of omniscience
or omnipotence in Mormon theology, or anywhere else, if we say that
God cannot know or do what absolutely cannot be known or done. In
fact, this is true by definition. Only those who would make of God an
ineffable mystery, a totally other being, incomprehensible and
uncomprehended, would suggest otherwise. Some writers may have
adopted such views. Even in Mormonism, if O. Kendall White is
correct, there exists such a temptation.[7] But if one chooses this
option, he or she must eschew rational theological investigation
because God will be a total mystery. This is not my position.

In orthodox Christian theology, Aquinas's position has become the standard view, and includes concepts which traditional Mormon theology rejects: that God is totally aloof from time; that time is his creation and his knowledge, power, and presence are extra-temporal. For God, there is no past, present, or future. These are human concepts and apply only to finite men and women. As Aquinas says, God's "knowledge is measured by eternity.... Things reduced to actuality in time are known by us successively in time, but by God they are known in eternity, which is above time."[8]

The relevant question for Mormons is whether we should adopt this teaching or something like it as our doctrine or whether a unique "finitistic" answer emerges from traditional Mormon theology. In the past most Mormon theologians seem to have advocated finitism. At present, however, some writers seem to be advancing a more absolutist view. For example, Mormon apostle Bruce R. McConkie wrote in 1980, "This great God, the Lord Almighty, ... is omnipotent, omniscient, and omnipresent. He has all power, knows all things, and by the power of his Spirit, is in and through all things."[9] To most, this definition would make God boundless in ways that equal, if not surpass, orthodox Christianity.

According to mainstream Christian thought, the only kind of omnipresent being that makes sense is one that is truly, as Paul Tillich put it, "the Ground of all Being" or "all-Being." Elder McConkie used the term in a different way. He said that God is everywhere present "by the power of his Spirit." Thus the Mormon view, according to Elder McConkie, is still one of a god who has a body, is located in time and space, and can influence all things by his spirit, whereas the traditional Christian view is one of a god who is only spirit or being and does not have spatial-temporal location.

A similar difference in definitions plagues the Mormon use of the term "omnipotence." In traditional Christian doctrine omnipotence can be used only when God—as the only necessary, eternally existing being—creates something out of nothing, including all the material elements, all souls, and all moral and natural laws. Everything else is dependent or contingent on God. In this context, God has all power because he can make all things come into or go out of existence. God's power is not limited in any way. But this is not the Mormon view. For Mormons, God "organized" previously existing elements according to certain principles or laws which are themselves independent of him and are to some extent out of his control. What Mormons mean when they use the word "omnipotent" is that God has all of the power that any being can have and that his power is sufficient to save humanity.

Mormon writers who use traditional Christian absolutist terms — such as "omniscience" and "omnipotence" — do not realize the extent to which Mormon theology differs from Catholic-Protestant theism. Such misapplication can be confusing to both Mormons and non-Mormons trying to understand Mormon teachings about the nature of God. But as McMurrin has pointed out, while some Mormons "sermonize with a language" of absolutism, only one view of time represents *the* traditional Mormon view[10] — namely, that "God himself is a temporal being with a past, present, and future, a being genuinely involved in the processes of the world."[11] In fact, Joseph Smith's 1844 King Follett Discourse, while not explicit on time, encourages a finitistic theology. Humanity is akin to God and Jesus Christ, for "God himself was once as we are *now*."[12] And since we are in time, so also are Christ and God.

Nineteenth- and early twentieth-century Mormon theologians Orson Pratt and B. H. Roberts both affirmed that God is in time. "The true God exists both in time and space," Pratt wrote. "He has extension, and form, and dimensions, as well as man. He occupies space; has a body, parts, and passions; can go from place to place — can eat, drink, and talk, as well as man."[13] Roberts stressed that God the son "became man," that there was for him a "before and after," and that "here there is a succession of time with God — a before and after; here is being and becoming."[14] Even knowledgeable non-Mormons assume that this is *the* Mormon position. Anglican theologian Edmond B. LaCherbonnier recently commented, "Mormons also conceive God as temporal, not eternal in the sense of timeless. This idea of a timeless eternity is incompatible with an acting God, for it would be static, lifeless, impotent. If God is an agent, then he must be temporal, for timeless action is a contradiction in terms."[15]

In contrast, Apostle Neal A. Maxwell recently articulated a different position: "Once the believer acknowledges that the past, present, and future are before God *simultaneously* — even though we do not understand how, then the doctrine of foreordination may be seen somewhat more clearly" (emphasis in original).[16] Realizing that this is probably difficult for most readers to understand, he explained, "When we mortals try to comprehend, rather than accept, foreordination, the result is one in which finite minds futilely try to comprehend omniscience."[17] Elder Maxwell suggested that God could not know what is in our future unless he is outside of time and knows all things simultaneously. Thus, God actually *sees* rather than *foresees* the future and is never surprised by what happens, although we often are. In support of this position, Elder Maxwell relied on several passages of scripture (see 1 Pet. 1:2; Moses 1:6; D&C 38:2; 1 Ne. 9:6; Al. 13:3).

Thus, if God is outside of time, then the past, present, and future are fictions since God's extra-temporal omniscience demands a simultaneous knowledge of the entire creation. A difficulty with this, however, is that all knowledge must occur co-temporaneously — that is, everything in creation must be occurring at the same time everywhere. While such a position can be maintained, I believe that it is inconsistent with the scriptural claim that God has foreknowledge. One has to decide whether God has simultaneous knowledge or whether he has true *fore*knowledge. For if God has foreknowledge, there is such a thing as "before"-knowledge and "after"-knowledge.[18]

One could adopt the view that foreknowledge is only from our mortal perspective but that for God there is no such thing as foreknowledge or foreordination. The difficulty here, however, is again that the scriptures themselves speak of the "foreknowledge" and the "foreordination" *of God*. As I read them there is no hint that these concepts apply only to humans or to our perspective. On the contrary, some passages of LDS scripture indicate that God is, in fact, both in time and space (see, for example, Moses 1:7; D&C 130:4). The position we are thus left in is clear: we can either assert the simultaneity of God's knowledge and abandon divine foreknowledge or we can assert divine foreknowledge which in some sense places God in time.[19]

Perhaps the biggest issue in the discussion of God's knowledge — whether it is extra-temporal and simultaneous or successive — is the question, Where does such a view leave the freedom and agency of men and women? Are we truly free to choose if God already knows what our choices and actions are? Some writers have asserted that just as a father can predict for his children how they will act and what they will do, so God, who has enormously greater knowledge than we do and who has known us over a much longer period of time, foresees all of our future acts.[20]

This is a common analogy, yet I believe it is faulty. The fundamental difficulty with it is that a father can only know in a general way based on his child's current dispositions and personality what that child will do in the future. He does not know when his child will do something, whether that thing will ever be done, or precisely in what way his child's character will be manifested. In other words, a father cannot know the specific future acts of his child. Furthermore, a father only knows what his child's future acts will be based on his knowledge of his child's current disposition. He does not claim to know what the future factors are that may change those dispositions.

If we use this analogy with God, we have to say, in order to make a claim for his total knowledge, that he not only knows our specific future acts but in addition has to know in advance every single influence which could alter our dispositional state and would know these now and simultaneously with everything else known, so that they would not lie in the future from God's perspective. But if we use such an argument, then the idea of human freedom is no longer coherent, for our apparent choices are not real choices and our freedom of action is only apparent.[21]

The issue is this: as Mormons we believe in freedom and free agency. In order for me to have freedom, I must have alternatives in my future that are *truly open* and not just *appear* to be open. Of course, I could think that I had alternatives when in fact God would know omni-temporally which alternative I would already select. But if it is the case that God knows that, then the future alternative choices I supposed to be open to me are not truly open. They are simply *apparent alternatives*. So, if God knows my every specific act, then I have no *real and meaningful* freedom.

The rebuttal is often made to this argument that God does not coerce or cause us to choose one alternative or another, and, therefore, we are still free even though God knows in advance which alternative we will select. I am willing to acknowledge the lack of coercion or force on God's part. But there is a *qualitative* change in the argument in moving from a father who is occasionally able to guess in a general way what his children will do in the future to God who knows all specific future acts and which are dated and located in time with regard to specific people. There is a profound difference between a father's *prediction* and God's totally accurate *knowledge*. This latter concept of knowledge is so strong that the analogy with the father breaks down completely. The difference between a father and God can be emphasized by saying that God is *never* surprised at anything.

In addition, given our free agency, it would be impossible for us ever to say, "We know that God expects us to be here on this day at this time doing what we are now doing, but we are going to reject this knowledge; we are going to attempt to foil God. We are going to rebel against what God knows as to what we will be doing here and now." For if God is totally omniscient, we must assert that he would know of our rebelliousness at this time and place. Of course, we could then say that if God knows of our rebelliousness, then we are not going to rebel; but then God would have known that also. In fact, it would be impossible for God to be surprised, disappointed, thrilled, exhilarated, or overjoyed with what we do, because he would have known what every one of us would do in every specific action we ever undertake, now and in all of the future. Again, this argument is incompatible with free agency.

If human freedom is compatible with God's omniscience—and there is no responsibility where there is no freedom—then we must choose which we consider to be more important: divine omniscience or human free agency and responsibility. Of course, one other alternative is to say: It is all a mystery and no one can understand how God can know in a totally omniscient way. But this is *not* an alternative I personally find attractive, because it seems to me that Mormon theology is commonsensical and rejects mainline Christian doctrines regarding the ineffability, incomprehensibility, and complete otherness of God.

Besides free agency, other Mormon doctrines are also incompatible with God's being completely outside of time. These include Mormonism's rejection of the traditional Christian concept of divine predestination; the belief that God experiences joy or happiness when his children obey his commandments or is angry or disappointed when they do not; the teaching that God is a personal being with body, parts, and passions; and the doctrine that we are of the same "race" as God. These, and other, ideas make up part of the very bulwark of Mormon theology, and essential to them is the position that God is not above time or space.

It is ironic that at a time when some Catholic and Protestant theologians are beginning to seriously question the attributes of divine absolutism in regard to human freedom, the problem of evil, and other issues,[22] Mormons who have not had to address these same dilemmas have begun to use absolutist terms. Mormons who are attracted to terms of absolutism should carefully consider what else they may unintentionally be embracing. They should consistently renounce such attributes or clearly distinguish between Mormon usage and traditional Christian usage. Unless this is done, I fear that absolutism may yet invade and perhaps change the uniqueness and very appeal of Mormon theology.

– NOTES –

1. See, for example, Ps. 44:21; Isa. 66:18; Luke 16:15; John 16:30; 1 Ne. 9:6; 2 Ne. 2:24; 9:20; W. of Mormon 1:7; D&C 38:2; Moses 1:6.

2. For the history and authorship of the "Lectures on Faith," see Leland H. Gentry, "What of the Lectures on Faith?" *Brigham Young University Studies* 19 (Fall 1978): 5–19. According to Elder Joseph Fielding Smith, the "Lectures on Faith" were removed from the Doctrine and Covenants because (1) they were never received by Joseph Smith as revelation; (2) they are only instructions regarding the general subject of faith and are not the official doctrine of the church; (3) their teachings regarding the Godhead are not complete; and (4) to avoid confusion on this point, they should not appear in the same volume as the commandments and revelations (quoted in John William Fitzgerald, "A Study of the Doctrine and Covenants," M.A. thesis, Brigham Young University, 1940, 343–45).

3. *Gospel Principles* (Salt Lake City: Church of Jesus Christ of Latter-day Saints, 1978), 6.

4. See Sterling M. McMurrin, *The Theological Foundations of the Mormon Religion* (Salt Lake City: University of Utah Press, 1965).

5. *Summa Theologica*, I, Q 14, Art. 9; hereafter ST.

6. In *The Deseret News*, 1911, 70.

7. See O. Kendall White, Jr., *Mormon Neo-Orthodoxy: A Crisis Theology* (Salt Lake City: Signature Books, 1987).

8. ST, Q 14, Art. 13.

9. Bruce R. McConkie, "The Lord God of the Restoration," *Ensign* 10 (Nov. 1980), 11:50, 51; see also Bruce R. McConkie, "The Seven Deadly

Heresies," typescript in my possession; and Bruce R. McConkie, "The Foolishness of Teaching," Church Educational System, 1981.

10. McMurrin, 35–40, *passim.*

11. Ibid., 13.

12. Joseph Fielding Smith, comp., *Teachings of the Prophet Joseph Smith* (Salt Lake City: Deseret Book, 1976), 345.

13. Orson Pratt, *The Kingdom of God* (Liverpool), 31 Oct. 1848, 48.

14. B. H. Roberts, *The Mormon Doctrine of Deity* (Salt Lake City, 1903), 95–96.

15. In Truman G. Madsen, ed., *Reflections on Mormonism, Judaeo-Christian Parallels* (Provo, UT: Brigham Young University Press, 1975), 157.

16. See Neal A. Maxwell, "A More Determined Discipleship," *Ensign* 9 (Feb. 1979), 2:69–73; and *All These Things Shall Give Thee Experience* (Salt Lake City: Deseret Book, 1979). See also my "Omnis on the Horizon," *Sunstone* 8 (July/Aug. 1983), 4:21–22, for additional discussion of omniscience in Mormon theology.

17. See Maxwell, "Discipleship," 70–71; see also Maxwell, *Experience*, 37.

18. See also Anthony Kenney, "Divine Foreknowledge and Human Freedom," in *Aquinas* (Garden City, NJ: Doubleday Anchor, 1969), 255–70.

19. For additional discussion of these points, see my "Time and Omniscience in Mormon Theology," *Sunstone* 5 (May/June 1980), 3:17–23. See also Gary James Bergera, "Grey Matters: Does God Progress in Knowledge," *Dialogue: A Journal of Mormon Thought* 15 (Spring 1982), 1:179–81.

20. See Maxwell, "Discipleship," 71, 72; Maxwell, *Experience*, 19, 20.

21. See Kenney.

22. See, for example, Anthony Kenny, *The God of the Philosophers* (Oxford: Clarendon Press, 1979), 121.

7.
The Concept of a Finite God as an Adequate Object of Worship

Blake T. Ostler

THE MOST COMMON CHALLENGE TO THE NOTION THAT GOD IS finite rather than infinite and absolute — that God is socially related with his creations and "in process" — is that such a being could not be perfect. Because what we generally mean by "God" is a being that is absolutely perfect and totally good, many people contend that solving the problem of evil by suggesting that God is not absolutely perfect denies that there is a God. This challenge to a finite God presupposes an idea of classical, absolutist perfection. The value judgment underlying this idea of absolute perfection was fostered by neo-Platonism which preferred Being to becoming, the One to the many, the timeless to the temporal, and the abstract Ideal to the concrete and material. The orthodox Christian notion of static or infinite and absolute perfection is that God exists completely independently of *any* relation to all other beings.

This concept of God's absolute sovereignty and independence, called aseity, consists of two aspects. First, if God is absolute then those attributes which are essential to his godly status cannot depend on anything independent of himself. Otherwise, he would be limited by dependence on other beings; and if they ceased to exist, he would cease to exist as God. Moreover, because God must be the explanation of all other existence, he must be absolutely unrelated to his creations. For if it were necessary to refer to any other thing to explain God, he would not be the unexplained explanation of the cosmos.

Second, the absolute must emulate all great-making attributes to their greatest potential, for anything potentially greater is not absolute. Hence, God must be completely actualized and therefore cannot progress in any manner, for unrealized potential is considered a defect. This line of reasoning is the basis for Aristotle's "Unmoved Mover" or Thomas Aquinas's "Actus Purus," a being who is "pure act" though without any act conceivably left to accomplish.

From these premises it follows that God is immutable and impassible, or unchanging in any way and without any feelings or passions. Aseity entails that God could not act to fulfill a need or enhance his status in any way. It also follows that creatures are simply superfluous to the Purely Actual God. God does not need creation; indeed, the very notion that God would undertake to create is inconsistent with the view that God is complete without any creatures. The notion of "sufficient reason" suggests that every positive action requires an explanation.[1] But what sufficient reason could God have to create anything if he has already accomplished everything and needs nothing? (While the criterion underlying this notion may never be proven, its validity is assumed by reason itself.) Unless God acted fortuitously in creating, then the criterion is reasonable and appears to entail that God would not undertake any positive action.

An all-good being would presumably prevent evil only if it could do so without thereby preventing some greater good not possible without the lesser evil. God would have created persons only out of his pure love for them and desire to enter into a genuine relationship with them. Love presupposes, however, an object that exists in some way. If God created persons out of love for them, they must have preexisted (at least in his foreknowledge) and in a mode more real than the manner in which ideas exist in the minds of mortals. Indeed, if God desired our love, then he manifested a need *essential* to godhood—but God's manifesting any need is clearly incompatible with the concept of an absolute being. What consistent meaning can be given to love when applied to a being that cannot respond, that cannot grow in happiness when others do or become sad when others experience sorrow? If God is loving he cannot be satisfied with the contemplation of his own perfection like the Aristotelian or Thomists' God.

The idea of static, absolute perfection must be replaced, I believe, with the idea of perfection as a dynamic creativity that acts to enhance the happiness of others and by so doing enhances its own happiness. As one non-Mormon theologian observed, "It is in fact extraordinary that Christian theologians have been so mesmerized by Greek [absolutist] concepts of perfection that they have been unable to develop a more truly Christian idea of God whose revealed nature is love."[2] The requirement that God must be unconditioned to be worthy of worship is unreasonable both because it is incoherent and because the being it describes is not available for religious purposes.

Faith requires that the object of its hope be minimally sufficient to bring about the realization of the maximally valuable state of affairs. The contemporary Mormon concept of a finite God *is* an adequate object of faith because all individuals, indeed all aspects of reality, look to him for the realization of all that matters most ultimately. The Mormon God is thus the Optimal Actualizer. God makes all things possible, but he can make all things actual only by working in conjunction with free individuals and actual entities. Hence, Mormonism does not shy away from recognizing humans as co-creators in God's purposes. God needs us and we need him for the realization of all that matters most. We are truly co-laborers, for growth of any nature or realized potential is impossible without him.

The Mormon revelation of a finite God also recognizes an immanent aspect of God's nature. Mormons refer to God's spirit to explain his influence or creative activity in the world. God stands in relation to his spirit as the sun stands in relation to the light emitted thereby, for it "proceedeth forth from the presence of God to fill the immensity of space" (D&C 88:12). Hence, even though God is confined to space and time by virtue of his corporeal aspect, he nevertheless acts upon and experiences all reality immediately by virtue of his spirit. God sustains the cosmos and has controlling power in the sense that his spirit is manifest in the creative moment of becoming in each actual entity. When his creative influence withdraws, the material universe consumes itself in entropy and individual atrophy, for his spirit is manifest in the "light which quickeneth your understandings. . . . The light which is in all things, which giveth life to all things, which is the law by which all things are governed" (D&C 88:7–13). Although God cannot determine how free entities will actualize the optimal options offered, without God's continual loving persuasion there are no genuine options. Hence, we properly praise and thank God for sustaining life and promoting personal growth.

The adequate object of worship must possess power sufficient to compensate for the possible eventualities brought about by the free choices of all beings, otherwise God's power and knowledge would be insufficient to insure the realization of his purposes. The Mormon plan of salvation is such a provision, compensating for the free choices of Adam (humankind) by meeting the eternal requirements of justice and mercy through the atonement of Jesus Christ. Although God is conditioned by eternal principles, he utilizes other eternal laws and principles to nullify their effect without contravening their efficacy, analogous to the way a jet utilizes natural laws to lift tons of steel into the atmosphere, overcoming the natural law of gravity without revoking it. Hence, God is an invincible ally who can insure the realization of his purposes. This has always been the Mormon understanding of God's omnipotence and miracles: not suspending natural laws but utilizing a complete knowledge of nature to accomplish what is not possible to mortals.

It should be noted that this concept of power appropriately places the emphasis on God as the object of religious worship and faith, for the point is not God's unlimited power and knowledge but his purposes and love. God need only possess power and knowledge sufficient to save, exalt, and insure the eternal lives of those who trust in him.[3] His knowledge and power certainly exceed this minimal requirement, but he is not thereby a more adequate object of faith. Indeed, the classical definitions of timeless omniscience and unlimited power are quite irrelevant to one aspiring to understand his relationship to deity. Religious faith is more a function of intimacy than of ultimacy, more a product of relationships than of logical necessities. That is why faith in God should make all the difference in the world.

Some may object to the attempt to understand the adequate object of faith because the absolute transcends all of our categories of thought. For many, to be mystified is to be edified and a God understood is a God unthroned. There is something dishonest, however, about a theology—any theology—which maintains that *reason* demands an absolute, infinite being as the adequate object of faith yet commits treason against reason whenever it speaks of God. God is not a more adequate object of faith simply because we attach to him contradictory notions of power, knowledge, timelessness, and aseity—adding nonsense to religious awe. In fact, if God is a total mystery, then we could never have any idea about the type of being it is, including whether it is an adequate object of faith or not. As David Hume's Cleanthes contended, "Religion would be better served were it to rest contented with more accurate and more moderate expressions. The terms *admirable, excellent, superlatively great, wise, and holy*— these sufficiently fill the imaginations of men, and anything beyond, besides that it leads to absurdities, has no influence on the affections or sentiments. . . . If we abandon all human analogy . . . I am afraid we abandon all religion and retain no conception of the great object of our devotion."[4]

In this sense, a finite God is uniquely worthy of worship. If the purpose of theology is to help mortals understand their relationship to God and the meaning of their experience in the world which surrounds them, then the least satisfying theology would be one that precludes a relationship between God and humanity or which takes refuge in mystery when confronted with human existence and our experience with evil.

The problem entailed in prayer to a finite being while worshipping absolute, infinite being is not exclusively Mormon; rather, it is a question which Christianity in general must face. The only truly absolute being is a pantheistic being, the identification of God with whatever is real. Judeo-Christians have pushed their concept of God as close as possible to pantheism to insure the absolute status of God. They have nevertheless shunned pantheism in name because it contravenes the teaching of Hebrew scripture that God is distinct from the world and socially involved with humans. Christians have insisted that God is personal yet possesses none of the characteristics common to persons. They have insisted that he is absolute, but not quite *that* absolute. They have asserted that God is both personal and absolute, yet what they propose is neither personal nor absolute. Therefore, Judeo-Christian theology fails to meet its own criteria of the adequate object of worship, for such a being is not the greatest conceivable being. In fact, it is not even a coherently conceivable being. Orthodox Christian theologians must abandon their theology when they kneel to address deity, and they must abandon the deity they pray to when they speak of theology. The acceptance of two mutually exclusive ideas has led to a dilemma in logic: A god that is both conditioned and unconditioned, related and unrelated, temporal and timeless. If Mormon Christianity is to remain true to its early Hebrew and Christian roots, I believe, its theology must be of a personal and therefore finite God who makes a difference in human experience.

– NOTES –

1. See Richard Taylor, *Metaphysics*, 2d ed. (Englewood Cliffs, NJ: Prentice Hall, Inc., 1974), 103–105.

2. Keith Ward, *Rational Theology and the Creativity of God* (Oxford: Basil Blackwell, 1982), 85.

3. David L. Paulsen, "The Comparative Coherency of Classical Theism and Mormon Finitism," Ph.D. diss., University of Michigan, 1975, 23.

4. David Hume, *Dialogues Concerning Natural Religion* (New York: Hafer Publishing, 1948), 71.

8.
Finitist Theology and the Problem of Evil

Peter C. Appleby
revised by Gary James Bergera

THE CHALLENGE WE CONFRONT IN ADDRESSING THE PROBLEM OF evil is demonstrating that faith in a good and benevolent god is not irrational in a world filled with injustice, suffering, and tragic death. The Lord rules over all, we are told, and is merciful; his providence extends to the least of his creatures. Yet a child is brutally decapitated, a young girl is raped, an old women is burned alive by terrorists, nearly half the people on earth never know a full and satisfying meal, and tens of thousands die each year of starvation and disease or otherwise suffer terribly in those natural disasters known as "acts of God." Under these circumstances, we must find some way of reconciling the existence of such evil with God's compassion and justice. As Boethius, the Roman philosopher, asked, "If there be a God, from whence proceed so many evils?"

Men and women of the orthodox Christian traditions have always been troubled by this question because their conception of God makes him a party to every event in the universe, including evil. This is not because he causes evil (though he has been so regarded by some people) but because he knows of every evil occurrence (since he is omniscient), because he has the power to prevent evil (since he is omnipotent), and because he is responsible for the overall structure and order of the universe (since he is its sole creator and sovereign). And since God's divine nature is unlimited, excuses such as

83

ignorance, incompetence, or conflicting obligations, which sometimes pardon ordinary persons, do not apply. In virtually every civi-
lization, individuals who do not render aid when they can are condemned as accessories to the evil they allow to occur. Thus God
would appear to be guilty under the principle that a moral agent is
at least partially responsible for any evil which he or she can know-
ingly prevent without causing a greater evil or seriously damaging
his or her own legitimate interests.

Believing Christians have responded to this with a variety of
arguments: some refuse to deal with the issue on theological
grounds, others attempt to show that God has sufficient reasons for
allowing evil to exist, and still others modify traditional teachings
about God to accommodate the observable facts. The first group
develops a line of thought suggested in the Book of Job that the ways
of God are not our ways, that divine goodness is unlike human
goodness, since the human mind can neither comprehend nor eval-
uate the divine character. Just as young children are unable to understand the motives of their parents, so human beings cannot comprehend the ways of God. And since we must accept, as an article of
faith, that God is perfectly good, he must have reasons for what he
does and permits, even though we cannot know what those reasons
are.

On the surface, this response seems plausible since God's
concerns and responsibilities must exceed ours and since honest
reflection requires us to admit that our mortal wisdom is severely
limited at best. But this response to the problem of evil is available
only at a price we cannot consistently pay, that of complete ignorance of God's values. In other contexts (prayer and preaching, for
example), we have definite beliefs about God, describing him as just,
merciful, and benevolent, and regard him as worthy of our love and
devotion. But if these positive qualities are to make sense, we must,
as John Stuart Mill and others have shown, attribute to God precisely
the same values—both positive and negative—that we accept ourselves. For if God's goodness is radically different from human goodness, there is little reason for calling it goodness at all and still less
for praising and glorifying it. The child who is totally ignorant of his
parents' values has no reason to admire or emulate them. Thus, the
problem of evil cannot be rationally evaded by pleading ignorance
of God's goodness.

A second and more promising response has been developed by a number of thoughtful writers, beginning with St. Augustine, who confront the issue directly, admitting its importance but arguing that God has sufficient reasons for creating a world filled with evil and allowing that evil to exist. Within this approach, the two most significant lines of thought are free will and eschatology, both of which attempt to show that divine ends can justify the means necessary for their realization, including a world of unrelieved tears for many of its inhabitants. Free will argues that the divine plan consists of developing a community of morally good persons who live in love and peace with one another and with God. But this can only emerge from the refining fires of temptation and free choice. This means that God must allow people to decide between good and evil, even though he knows that many of them will choose the latter. Innocence could be maintained without freedom, since a person who is unable to choose can do no wrong. But innocence is not goodness. And if real moral worth is the goal, freedom and the risk of disaster are the inescapable price. For even omnipotence cannot guarantee that true freedom will always be used constructively. Thus, in order to develop a moral community, God allows us to decide freely despite the tragic consequences of many of our decisions.

Free will is complemented by eschatology, which attempts to account for suffering in this world by invoking heavenly rewards and compensations. Ours is a world in which innocence suffers and evil prospers, and accident, disease, and disaster fall upon the just as well as the unjust. But all will be made right in the divine kingdom beyond the grave. There the righteous will be rewarded, the innocent compensated, and the celestial community will be forever free from misery, travail, and death. Mortal life is a period of trial and testing, while life in the world to come sees the realization of justice, benevolence, and abundance promised to those who suffer undeservedly. The goodness of God is vindicated by the nobility of his purpose in the present world and the justice of the next.

Once again this seems plausible, but as soon as we recall that God presumably originated the entire arrangement, it is no longer clear that either argument supports the claim that he is just. Eschatology portrays him as generous with those who have suffered through no fault of their own but does not justify their being victimized in the first place. Nor does it suggest what could be fair and just compensation for the evils of this life. It does predict that the lion will finally lie down with the lamb, but it gives no hint as to how the lamb could find justice in such an arrangement. If God allowed people to suffer at all, the fact that he rewarded them later might show him to be generous or ultimately compassionate, but it would not show him to be just and good always.

Free will portrays God as engaging in a noble experiment, setting us free to determine our own moral destinies and allowing us real opportunities to make decision. But it does not show why it is necessary to allow us to commit horrendous crimes against one another or to perpetuate gross injustices from generation to generation. Nor does it explain the inequitable distribution of trials and temptations, which leaves some lives in relative peace and prosperity, while others are permanently scarred and disfigured. Christians sometimes say that the Lord requires no one to carry a cross which is heavier than he or she can bear. Even if this were true, it would not be clear why some crosses are so much heavier than others or why some especially terrible crosses must be borne at all. The ends of this divine experiment may thus be noble and elevating, but the means by which they are realized are in no sense just and good.

In view of these and other difficulties, we seem unable to modify traditional teachings about God to accommodate the obvious facts of the case. For if God is just and good, he is not responsible for the specific conditions in which we work out our moral destinies and he is not morally involved with the evils afflicting human life. I would argue that theological finitism, which challenges orthodox claims of God's omnipotence, omniscience, and status as cosmic architect, can accomplish this but only by "demythologizing" much that is said in the Bible and elsewhere about the activities of God. Finitism can, I believe, maintain a religiously adequate conception of God, holding him to be the ultimate locus and example of love and creativity, but requires that we abandon the stories of mighty acts, which form much of the core of orthodox Christianity.

First, we must deny that God is solely or primarily responsible for the design and creation of our world, since that world is so unjust and unmerciful to many, if not most, of its inhabitants. There are independent reasons for rejecting the notion of a divine architect, as David Hume and others have shown. But if we were to insist upon the idea of a designer, we might hold that God is one of a cluster of coequal powers responsible for the organization of the universe under conditions which precluded any one of them from achieving dominance over the others. In this way, the desirable features of the universe could be attributed to God, while the rest could be placed at the door of forces he could not control. Or finitism might see God simply as the source of spirituality, love, and creativity and maintain that there are signs of God's influence throughout the structure and history of the world, wherever positive values prevail over the forces of darkness. Here, with the literal doctrine of creation being given up, the ancient idea of "man in the image of God" might be reinterpreted to mean that humans reflect the divine nature to the extent that they are capable of intelligence, creativity, and love.

The second finitist requirement involves the curtailment of traditional claims about divine power, denying omnipotence and insisting that God has none of the miraculous powers attributed to him in Christian literature. For the problem of evil is incompatible with any deity possessing such powers. There are simply too many avoidable agonies in our world to allow that a just and benevolent God has the ability to intervene but refrains from doing so except on rare and unpredictable occasions. Accordingly, finitist theology argues that God has only those powers which are inherent in the perfect love and creative intelligence that are his essential characteristics. God's way is not that of forceful and dramatic moving and shaking but of subtle attraction and gentle persuasion. And there is more than a little biblical support for the belief that loving, non-resistance to evil is ultimately the greatest power in the world.

Finally, with respect to omniscience, finitism need not deny that God knows all that can be known but rather that the range of possible knowledge is more restricted than orthodoxy admits. Thus, we may well accept the idea that God is comprehensively aware of all that takes place in the world. But we deny that God has infallible knowledge of every future occurrence, because this conflicts with the view that moral agents are free in their decisions. And we may well believe that God possesses a perfect understanding of the laws governing the behavior of everything which moves, changes, or acts. But we reject the tendency to cast God in the role of a cosmic forecaster who could, and therefore should, warn victims of impending misfortune. Whatever the content of God's mind and however that content might be assembled, its contents cannot be available to human minds on pain of reintroducing the problem of evil. Nor can it include full knowledge of the future on pain of denying freedom. But if these qualifications are allowed, there is no reason for denying it the name of omniscience.

These revisions, of course, would affect some familiar religious discourse. They would deny the orthodox Christian doctrine of the Creation and Fall in order to avoid the charge that God deliberately condemned half of humanity as a means of teaching moral lessons to the other half. They would eliminate stories of supernatural miracles because such power otherwise breeds responsibility for such apparent divine omissions as God's failure to turn away the wrath of Adolf Hitler before the holocaust. And they would reject the view of the divine mind as a limitless repository of information to be dealt out at random intervals to a few individuals, since this idea of omniscience cannot explain why more than two dozen boys and young men had to die before the Atlanta, Georgia, police were able to find their murderer. In short, these revisions would sacrifice divine power to defend divine goodness, revering the ancient vision which saw God as love.

I know of no theologian or philosopher today—Mormon or otherwise—who actually espouses the precise finitist doctrine I have proposed here. The virtues I claim for it are just two: it avoids the problem of evil and it responds to some of the sensibilities of religious tradition. If we conceive of God as that being which is uniquely worthy of worship, it might well be worth considering how loyal we should remain to the adoration of sheer power.

9.
The Development of the Concept of a Holy Ghost in Mormon Theology

Vern G. Swanson

APOSTLE JOSEPH FIELDING SMITH ONCE ADMONISHED ALL Latter-day Saints not to theorize on the subject of the Holy Ghost. "We should have no time to enter into speculation in relation to the Holy Ghost," he wrote. "Why not leave a matter which in no way concerns us alone."[1] Of all the so-called "mysteries" the subject of the Holy Ghost has been one of the most taboo and hence least studied. Church writers have published prolifically on the operations and gifts of the Holy Ghost, but they have had little to say regarding his origin, identity, and destiny.[2]

In contrast to this lack of analysis, I will consider the development since 1830 of notions about the Holy Ghost. Joseph Smith may have received and imparted understanding "line upon line," but the absence of any thorough-going commentary has led to strong differences of opinion as to the identity and nature of the Holy Ghost.

The Book of Mormon and early sections of the Doctrine and Covenants presented a kind of monotheistic trinitarian view of the Holy Ghost (2 Ne. 31:21; Al. 11:44; 3 Ne. 11:27–28, 36; 28:10; Morm. 7:7).[3] The major Christian sects in 1830 taught the Athanasian Creed: "One God in Trinity, and Trinity in Unity, neither confounding the persons: nor dividing the Substance." Sectarian understanding tended toward the term "Holy Spirit" rather than "Holy Ghost"

and dealt less with the person of the Holy Ghost than with its attributes and operations.

In March and April 1830 the "laying on of hands for the gift
of the Holy Ghost" was officially coupled in Mormon ritual with
water baptism (D&C 19:31; 20:43). The laying on of hands for the
bestowal of spiritual gifts was common during the 1830s, but this
coupling with baptism was fairly controversial (Acts 2:28; 8:17; 19:6;
Heb. 6:12). However, the definition of the nature of the Holy Spirit at
this time was still basically sectarian and triune: " ... which Father,
Son and Holy Ghost are one God, infinite and eternal, without end"
(D&C 20:28).

The nature of the Holy Spirit was first discussed in Mormon
thought about 1835. The "Lectures on Faith," bound with the 1835
edition of the Doctrine and Covenants, included the following:
"There are two personages who constitute the great matchless, governing and supreme power over all things ... The Father and the
Son — the Father being a personage of spirit, glory and power, possessing all perfection and fullness, the Son ... a personage of tabernacle, made or fashioned like unto a man ... possessing the same
mind with the Father, which *mind* is the Holy Spirit."[4]

This document was sanctioned as the official position of the
church throughout the Kirtland and Missouri periods and beyond.
According to Thomas G. Alexander, "This view of the Holy Ghost [as
the mind of the Father and the Son] reinforced trinitarian doctrine
by explaining how personal beings like the Father and Son become
one God through the non-corporeal presence of a shared *mind*."[5]
The Holy Ghost in this binitarian understanding was the "mind" or
common essence, the "Spirit of God" and the "Light of Christ,"
emanating from the Father and Son. Most literature from this early
period emphasized the "influence," "power," "fire," "spirit," and
"gifts" of the Holy Ghost. It was something to be "spread," "filled,"
"poured," or "bestowed" upon the righteous, especially after baptism.

The next stage in Mormon concepts of a Holy Ghost was
signalled in June 1839 when Joseph Smith explained that the Second
Comforter was Jesus Christ and the First Comforter was the Holy
Ghost.[6] Though not a major revision, this statement proposed a
particular relationship between Jesus and the Holy Ghost which had

not previously been emphasized. However, Smith continued to call the Holy Ghost "It" and generally dealt with the topic as the "Lectures on Faith" had.

Not until February 1841 did Smith explicitly refer to the Holy Ghost as an individual spirit person: "Joseph said concerning the Godhead, it was not as many imagined — three heads and but one body — he said the three were separate *bodies* — God the first and Jesus the Mediator the second and the Holy Ghost and these three agree in one."[7] Here for the first time Smith proclaimed a "homoiusion" existence for the Holy Ghost: it had a separate body. But this was a veiled comment given before a small group of Mormons in Nauvoo, Illinois, and only William P. McIntire's "Minute Book" recorded the statement. Three weeks later McIntire recorded an even more explicit reference to the Holy Ghost: "However there is a priesthood with the Holy Ghost [a] Key — the Holy Ghost overshadows you and witnesses unto you of the authority and gifts of the Holy Ghost. . . . The Son [has] a tabernacle and so had the Father, but the Holy Ghost is a personage of spirit without [a] tabernacle."[8]

Joseph Smith may have spoken of the Holy Ghost in these terms earlier than 1841, but no records have survived that would indicate he had. However, in June 1844 Smith himself claimed that he had distinguished three separate personages in the Godhead from the beginning of his restoration movement: "I wish to declare I have always and in all congregations, when I have preached, it has been the plurality of Gods, it has been preached 15 years. I have always declared God to be a distinct personage, Jesus Christ a separate and distinct personage from God the Father [and] the Holy Ghost was a distinct personage and separate and these three constitute three distinct personages and three Gods."[9] This statement, made the same month Smith was assassinated, remains his most explicit "tritheistic" explanation of the Trinity.

The earliest available public statement of the doctrine of the individuality of the Holy Ghost came a year earlier in January 1843 when Smith publicly taught that the "Holy Ghost is a personage in the form of a personage."[10] On 15 May 1843 the *Times and Seasons* published the substance of this discourse. There Smith explained that the "Sign of the Dove," which six months earlier he had referred to in the Book of Abraham (fac. 3, fig. 7), was the "Sign" of the Holy

Ghost not the Holy Ghost himself. As the third member of the Godhead, the Holy Ghost, Smith said, is a being in the form and shape of a person.

The statement which three decades later found its way into Mormon scripture as section 130 of the Doctrine and Covenants came in April 1843 at Ramus, Illinois. That Sunday Smith "instructed" William Clayton, Orson Hyde, and others: "The Holy Ghost is a personage and a person cannot have the personage of the Holy Ghost in his heart."[11] William Clayton's diary was later amended by Willard Richards for Joseph Smith's diary and was probably revised by Church Historian George A. Smith and Thomas Bullock into the version which appeared in the "Manuscript History of the Church" by November 1854: "The Father has a body of flesh and bones as tangible as man's; the Son also, but the Holy Ghost has not a body of flesh and bones, but is a personage of spirit."

Such statements corrected the notion that the Holy Ghost was a spirit essence and not an actual spirit person. By the time of his death in June 1844, Joseph Smith's beliefs about the personal reality of the Holy Ghost had been clearly articulated, at least to a few. However, this had not been communicated unambiguously to the Saints at large. Even the apostles, who were mostly on missions during the later Nauvoo period, had not always been kept current on Smith's developing theology. John Taylor, for example, lingered with the old interpretation of "two living Gods and the Holy Ghost for this world."[12]

Uncertainty remained into the Utah period. Apostle Orson Pratt seemed unsure about whether the Holy Ghost had a personal or diffused nature. His address of 18 February 1855 vacillated between both views: "But I will not say that the Holy Ghost is a personage. . . . I will tell you what I believe in regard to the Holy Ghost's being a person; but I know of no revelation that states that this is the fact, neither is there any that informs us that it is not the fact, so we are left to form our own conclusions upon the subject. . . . It is in fact, a matter of doubt with many, and of uncertainty, I believe, with all, whether there is a personal Holy Spirit or not . . . consequently I cannot fully make up my mind one way or the other."[13]

That same year, Orson's brother, Apostle Parley P. Pratt, published his *Key to the Science of Theology*, which emphasized a non-personal Holy Ghost who was an omnipresent spirit.[14] A year later

Orson Pratt printed in England the pamphlet *The Holy Ghost*. His views there echoed those of his 1855 address. Some ten years later in 1865 this pamphlet was officially condemned for indulging in "hypotheses and theories, he has launched forth on an endless sea of speculation to which there is no horizon."[15]

It may have been the difficulties with Orson Pratt which led Brigham Young, George A. Smith, and Wilford Woodruff to print Joseph Smith's revelation of April 1843. The Manuscript History was serialized in the *Deseret News,* and the section containing the expanded version of the prophet's revelation was printed on 9 July 1856.[16] It was later republished in the *Millennial Star* on 13 November 1858 and would eventually become Doctrine and Covenants 130.

At the time, Joseph Smith's expanded revelation evidently had little impact on the views of many Saints. In 1852, for example, Brigham Young preached: "The Holy Ghost is the Spirit of the Lord, and issues forth from Himself, and may properly be called God's minister to execute His will in immensity; being called to govern by His influence and power; but He is not a person of tabernacle as we are and as our Father in Heaven and Jesus are."[17] Five years later he similarly argued: "Least you should mistake me, I will say that I do not wish you to understand that the Holy Ghost is a personage having a tabernacle like the Father and the Son; but he is God's messenger that diffuses his influence through all the works of the Almighty."[18] Since Young twice allowed the printing of Smith's 1843 revelation during these years, one assumes that he saw no conflict between his own views and those of Smith.

What was at stake in passages such as those quoted above was the distinction between the kinds of bodies possessed by personages in the Godhead. There was little attempt to clarify ambiguities until Apostle Joseph F. Smith declared in 1876: "The Holy Ghost is a personage who acts in Christ's stead."[19] At the same conference section 130 was officially canonized as part of the Doctrine and Covenants. (The editing of the new 1876 edition of the Doctrine and Covenants had been done by Orson Pratt under the direction of Brigham Young.) The late Nauvoo teachings of Joseph Smith on the Holy Ghost had finally become "official" church doctrine.

However, the old understanding still continued, as in, for example, John Jaques's *Catechism for Children: Exhibiting the Prominent Doctrines* (1877) and B. H. Roberts's *The Gospel* (1888). Roberts was later influenced by James E. Talmage's lectures and writings on the subject and, by the third edition of *The Gospel* in 1901, had moved to a more literal interpretation of the Holy Ghost.[20] Two years later, when he published *Mormon Doctrine of Deity*, Roberts clearly expressed the contemporary understanding promoted by Joseph F. Smith and James Talmage.

At least three factors contributed to the longevity of the idea that the Holy Ghost was not a personage, more a "part" rather than a "member" of the Godhead: the scarcity of Nauvoo documents making clear Joseph Smith's later teachings; the recalcitrance of George Q. Cannon of the First Presidency; and the continued inclusion of the "Lectures on Faith" in editions of the Doctrine and Covenants. Because of this, Mormons tended to rely on Kirtland-period theology, retreating to established sources and conventions.

However, at least one scriptural passage seemed all along to argue for the Holy Ghost as a personage of spirit. Book of Mormon prophet Nephi had written: "For I spake unto him as a man speaketh; for I beheld that he was in the form of a man; yet nevertheless, I knew that it was the spirit of the Lord; and he spake unto me as a man speaketh with another" (1 Ne. 11:11). Orson Pratt was unsure of the identity of the "Spirit of the Lord" mentioned in this verse, "Whether the spirit that Nephi saw in the form of a man was the person of the Holy Ghost or the personal spirit of Jesus."[21] Later James Talmage and B. H. Roberts confirmed that the spirit had been the Holy Ghost.[22]

The second factor was George Q. Cannon, who noted in 1883 — after the adoption of section 130 — "that there were two personages of the Godhead, two presiding personages whom we worship and to whom we look, the one the Father and the other the Son."[23] Cannon most likely objected to Talmage's discussions of the Holy Ghost. In 1894–95 Talmage had given a series of doctrinal addresses on the Godhead at the Latter-day Saints University. These became the basis for his book, *Articles of Faith.*[24] Talmage recorded in his diary Cannon's comments about the book's treatise on the Holy Ghost in January 1899: "Commenting on the ambiguity existing in our printed works concerning the nature or character of the Holy Ghost, [Cannon] expressed his opinion that the Holy Ghost was in reality a person, in the image of the other members of the

Godhead—a man in form and figure; and that what we often speak of as the Holy Ghost is in reality but the power or influence of the spirit. . . . [However, the First Presidency] deemed it wise to say as little as possible on this as on other disputed subjects."[25]

Only a month earlier, Cannon had made his longstanding views on the Godhead perfectly clear in his speech, "Things that should and things that should not be taught in our Sunday Schools": "The Lord has said through his Prophet that there are two person-ages in the Godhead. That ought to be sufficient for us at the present time. I have heard during my life a great many speculations concern-ing the personage of the Holy Ghost—whether he was a personage or not. But it has always seemed to me that we had better not en-deavor to puzzle ourselves or allow our minds to be drawn out upon questions of this kind, concerning which the Lord has not revealed perhaps all that we desire. When men give themselves licence to do this, they are very apt to be led along into error and imbibe ideas that are not sound."[26]

Cannon lived only two more years, and his death made it easier for younger theologians to assert themselves. The reconstruc-tion of Mormon doctrine was in full swing with the publication of John A. Widtsoe's *A Rational Theology*, Roberts's *Seventies Course in Theology*, and Talmage's *Jesus the Christ*. Also by 1915 Apostle Charles W. Penrose had completed his revision of Pratt's *Key to the Science of Theology*. Without noting his alterations, Penrose deleted or changed passages describing the Holy Ghost as a non-personal "spiritual fluid" pervading the universe.[27] This new emphasis was made "official"when the First Presidency asked Talmage to draft an offi-cial statement on the Godhead which the church issued in 1916.[28] The declaration made it clear that there were two corporeal beings and one personage of spirit in the Godhead.

The third problem which complicated the development of the doctrine of the Godhead was the presence of the "Fifth Lecture on Faith" in the Doctrine Covenants. By November 1917 the First Presidency and twelve were considering a revision of the lectures. In the end a committee was established to revise the entire Doctrine and Covenants.[29] The "Lectures on Faith" were deleted and classi-fied as "non-scriptural" even though the 1835 April conference of the church had accepted them as authoritative and binding. With the

1921 edition of the Doctrine and Covenants, Joseph Smith's later doctrinal understanding of the Holy Ghost finally superceded earlier explanations.

The disagreement about whether the Holy Ghost was personal or impersonal had clearly been at the center of discussion for over eighty years. But other concepts about the identity of the Holy Ghost are still being debated today. Two little-known journal accounts from the Nauvoo period suggest that Joseph Smith may have taken the idea of an anthropomorphic Holy Ghost far, conjecturing that the Holy Ghost is a messiah or savior in training for another world. This notion implies that Jesus Christ was a holy ghost for a previous system or generation. Even though this concept seems new to contemporary Latter-day Saints, there are no official doctrines with which it conflicts.

According to this view, the position or calling of "Holy Ghost" is one of service, experience, and preparation for the future. According to an account of a 27 August 1843 sermon by the founding prophet, "Joseph also said that the Holy Ghost is now in a state of probation, which if he should perform in righteousness he may pass through the same or a similar course of things the Son has."[30] George Laub's account of an 16 June 1844 sermon, just before the martyrdom, echoes this earlier account: "But the Holy Ghost is yet a spiritual body and waiting to take to himself a body, as the Saviour did or as God (the Father) did, or the gods before them took bodies. For the Saviour says the works that My Father did do I also, and these are the works, He took a body and then laid down His life that he might take it up again."[31]

Elsewhere Smith apparently taught that God the Father had once been a savior and that Jesus Christ will be a "God the Father" for his own generation of spirit offspring.[32] Brigham Young likewise taught that there is more than one savior: "Sin is upon every earth that ever was created. . . . Consequently every earth has its redeemer and every earth has its tempter; and every earth and the people thereof . . . pass through all the ordeals that we are passing through."[33] And John Taylor indicated that our Godhead was for this particular system, implying that there were other systems and other godheads: "Our Father in Heaven and who with Jesus Christ, his First Begotten Son, and the Holy Ghost, are one in power, one in dominion and one in glory, constituting the First Presidency of this system and this Eternity."[34] It seems possible that Joseph Smith believed that the members of the Godhead eventually experience each position in the divine presidency as God the third, then God the second, and finally God the first.

There are other theories regarding the identity of the Holy Ghost attributed to Joseph Smith. The most widespread is the belief that Smith was the Holy Ghost; or more correctly stated, that he represented the emanating spirit of the Father and the Son.[35] This theory arose from several sources. In a 9 March 1841 discourse Joseph Smith apparently discussed three gods who covenanted to preside over this creation: "[An] Everlasting Covenant was made between three personages before the organization of this earth, and [it] relates to their dispensation of things to men on the earth."[36] These three gods, some argue, were Father Adam for the beginning of the mortal world, Christ for the Meridian of Time, and Joseph Smith for the Dispensation of the Fullness of Times. Others have seen Doctrine and Covenants 135:3 as evidence for Smith being the Holy Ghost: "Joseph Smith, the Prophet and Seer of the Lord, has done more, save Jesus only, for the salvation of men in this world than any other man that ever lived in it." Accordingly, Christ did the most to save humanity and is the second member of the Godhead; therefore, Smith, who did second to the most, is the third member.

That such notions have circulated in the church since 1844 is made clear by comments from church leaders contradicting these views. In August 1845 Orson Pratt wrote to church members responding to rumors that Joseph Smith was the Holy Ghost incarnate: "Let no false doctrine proceed out of your mouth, such, for instance that the tabernacle of our martyred prophet and seer, or of any other person, was or is the especial tabernacle of the Holy Ghost, in a different sense from that considered in relation to his residence in other tabernacles. These are doctrines not revealed, and are neither believed nor sanctioned by the Twelve and should be rejected by every Saint."[37]

Similarly, in January 1845, Brigham Young responded to conjectures about what Joseph Smith may have meant when Smith said, "Would to God, brethren I could tell you who I am! Would to God I could tell you what I know! But you would call it blasphemy and want to take my life."[38] Young specifically countered any interpretation that Smith was the Holy Ghost: "[Y]ou have heard Joseph say that the people did not know him; he had his eyes on the relation to blood-relations. Some have supposed that he meant spirit [Holy Ghost], but it was the blood-relation. This is it that he referred to. His descent from Joseph that was sold into Egypt was direct and the blood was pure in him."[39]

Other theories circulate in the church. According to one, the Holy Ghost will be the last person born on the earth at the end of the Millennium. He will receive his body last so that he may be of service to all until the end. Another theory holds that the spirits of all good people who have died become Holy Ghosts (plural).[40] Others argue that Adam or Michael is the Holy Ghost.[41] Another names Abel as the Holy Ghost, another the Angel Gabriel. Notions such as the latter three assume the Holy Ghost is a "Spirit of a Just Man made Perfect" rather than a pre-mortal spirit. Increasingly popular is the idea that Mother in Heaven is the Holy Ghost. There are no known sources in Latter-day Saint literature to support this final idea but precedent in ancient religions abounds.

In the end, there are few details from which to construct an adequate theology of God the Third. I hope that this essay will encourage more research on the subject. But I suspect that we will be left at some point with Brigham Young's promise that "when we go through the veil we shall know much more about these matters than we now do."[42]

— NOTES —

1. Joseph Fielding Smith, "How Can a Spirit be a Member of the Godhead?" *Answers to Gospel Questions* (Salt Lake City: Deseret Book, 1958), 2:145.

2. Major published works on this topic are Oscar W. McConkie, *The Holy Ghost* (Salt Lake City: Deseret Book, 1952); N. B. Lundwall, *Discourses of the Holy Ghost* (Salt Lake City: Bookcraft, 1959); Duane S. Crowther, *Gifts of the Spirit* (Salt Lake City: Bookcraft, 1965). Other publications include B. H. Roberts, "The Holy Ghost," in *The Seventy's Course in Theology* (1912), 6–114. Perhaps the one church leader who wrote the most on this topic was Orson Pratt; see Brigham Young et al., *Journal of Discourses*, 26 vols. (Liverpool: S. W. Richards, 1855–86), 2 (18 Feb. 1855): 337–45; hereafter JD.

3. Van Hale, "Defining the Mormon Doctrine of Deity," *Sunstone* 10 (Jan. 1985): 23–27, reprinted in the present compilation. The word "trinitarian" is used here to note that early converts to the church were able

to apply their existing understanding of the Godhead to Book of Mormon verses. Some "Mormon" churches have returned to the Book of Mormon concept of one god only.

4. "Lectures on Faith" (Kirtland, OH, 1835), 48. This comes from the fifth lecture.

5. Thomas G. Alexander, "The Reconstruction of Mormon Doctrine from Joseph Smith to Progressive Theology," *Sunstone* 5 (July-Aug. 1980): 26; also see Boyd Kirkland, "Jehovah as the Father," *Sunstone* 8 (1984): 44, and "Elohim and Jehovah," *Dialogue* 19 (Spring 1986): 77-78; all reedited and reprinted in the present compilation.

6. Andrew Ehat and Lyndon Cook, *Words of Joseph Smith* (Salt Lake City: Bookcraft, 1980), 4. See John 14: 12-17 and D&C 88:3-4.

7. Ibid., 63.

8. Ibid., 64.

9. Ibid., 378.

10. Ibid., 160.

11. Ibid., 170.

12. John Taylor, *Times and Seasons*, 15 Feb. 1845, 253. See also Jesse Haven, "Some of the Principle Doctrines (1853)," in David J. Whittaker, "Early Mormon Imprints in South Africa," *Brigham Young University Studies* 20:411: "We believe the personage of God is filled with the Holy Ghost, and this Holy Ghost or Spirit of God is diffused through all space and by this spirit, God is everywhere present holding the works of his hands."

13. JD 2:337-38. Also see Orson Pratt, *Millennial Star* 12 (1851):308: "We are not there informed whether the third, called the Holy Spirit is a personage or not."

14. Parley P. Pratt, *Key to the Science of Theology* (Salt Lake City, 1855).

15. Orson Pratt, "The Holy Spirit," *Orson Pratt New Series* (1856), 55-64. This pamphlet is a revision of his earlier articles, "The Holy Spirit," *Latter-day Saints' Millennial Star*, 15 Oct. 1850, 305-309; 1 Nov. 1850, 325-28. The condemnation came as a "Proclamation of the First Presidency and Twelve" in the *Millennial Star*, 21 Oct. 1865.

16. *Deseret News*, 9 July 1856, 137. Parley P. Pratt died soon thereafter without making revisions to his book, *Key to the Science of Theology*. This popular book continued in its present form until the early twentieth century, when Charles W. Penrose revised it.

17. JD 1:50.

18. Ibid., 6:95.

19. Ibid., 18:275. Smith felt that there were two aspects of the Holy Ghost or Spirit: (1) an omnipresent light of "pure intelligence" and (2) a representative of this "pure intelligence," a male personage of spirit who holds the office of "Holy Ghost." In the intervening years, the

"Proclamation" condemning some of Orson Pratt's teachings had been issued.

20. B. H. Roberts, *The Gospel: An Exposition of its First Principles* (Salt Lake City, 1888). Pages 212 and 214 were retained in the 1901 edition, but a new paragraph was added to explain that the Holy Ghost was a spiritual personage (p. 199). The question as to how anyone could believe that the Holy Ghost was a diffuse spirit after D&C 130 was canonized was answered by B. H. Roberts who interpreted this scripture along the lines of the old interpretation: " . . . Holy Ghost, whose tabernacle is in the elements of the universe, giving life and light and intelligence to all things and is the grand medium of communication between God the Father and His Son Jesus Christ and their vast creations" (p. 214, 1888 edition). Thus was the scripture interpreted completely opposite from its interpretation today.

21. *Millennial Star*, 15 Oct. 1850, 306–308. See also Eth. 3:6–16 and D&C 107:56.

22. Talmage, *Articles of Faith* (Salt Lake City: Deseret News, 1899), 164–65, and Roberts, *The Seventy's Course in Theology* (1912), 60–61.

23. JD 24:372.

24. Lyndon Cook theorizes that Talmage may have used Abraham H. Cannon as a "conduit" to his father, George Q. Cannon, while Talmage was a professor at the Latter-day Saint University. Talmage thought it important to codify and clarify ambiguity of doctrines. See *Juvenile Instructor* 29 (1 April 1894): 220. Alexander, "Reconstruction of Mormon Doctrine," credits Talmage with almost singlehandedly developing the modern Mormon concept of the Holy Ghost (p. 28). The importance of George A. Smith and Joseph F. Smith must also be considered — as, for example, the following statement: "The Holy Ghost is a personage in the Godhead, and is not that which lighteth every man that comes into the world." *Improvement Era* 11: 380–82.

25. Talmage journal, 5 Jan. 1899, Special Collections, Harold B. Lee Library, Brigham Young University, Provo, Utah.

26. George Q. Cannon, *Proceedings of the First Sunday School Convention* (Salt Lake City: Deseret Sunday School Union, 1899), 87. Cannon was then first counselor to church president Lorenzo Snow and general superintendent of the Sunday school. Talmage would not become an apostle until 1911. Cannon gave this speech during a conference held on 28–29 November 1898. Cannon may have changed his mind about the Holy Ghost being a personage, but Talmage's summary of their conversation does not necessarily prove such a change.

27. Anthon H. Lund journal, 21 Jan. 1915, archives, Church of Jesus Christ of Latter-day Saints. See Parley P. Pratt's *Key to the Science of Theology* (fifth edition). According to Alexander, "Reconstruction of Mormon

Doctrine," pages 68, 75, 100–102, and 139 were "corrected"; the seventh edition saw further revisions on pages 48, 66, 73, 92–94, and 100.

28. "The Father and the Son: A Doctrinal Exposition by the First Presidency and the Twelve" (1916), in James R. Clark, ed., *Messages of the First Presidency* (Salt Lake City: Bookcraft, 1971), 5:23–24.

29. Heber J. Grant journal, 21 Jan. 1917 and 20 Aug. 1921, church archives. See also Alexander, 33n38.

30. Ehat and Cook, 245.

31. Ibid., 305. "The gods before them" seems to refer to God's father rather than to his exalted brothers and sisters.

32. Ibid., 345. See also Amasa Lyman, JD 7:297: "Know the history of the Father, learn it in the Son. . . . He came [to] do the works which he saw His Father do."

33. See JD 14:71–72. Brigham Young also taught that devils are on all earths that pass through the same ordeals as ours (ibid., 9:108).

34. John Taylor, *Mediation and Atonement* (Salt Lake City: Deseret News, 1882), 76. This statement first appeared in Taylor's editorial for the *Times and Seasons*, 15 Feb. 1845. It was a response to W. W. Phelps's editorial of 1 January. Taylor's statement seems to imply that there are twelve inhabited planets for each eternity, as well.

35. See Francis M. Darter, *The Holy Ghost is Who and What?* (Salt Lake City, 1938), 13; and Fred C. Collier, "The Trinity and The Holy Spirits: The Doctrine as Joseph Taught It," *Doctrine of the Priesthood* 5 (1 April 1988).

36. Ehat and Cook, 87–88n5.

37. Orson Pratt, "Message," *Times and Seasons* 6 (15 Aug. 1845): 809. This is a reprint of Pratt's letter to the *New York Messenger*.

38. Orson F. Whitney, *The Life of Heber C. Kimball* (Salt Lake City: Bookcraft, 1945), 333. See also Brigham Young, JD 9:294: "If I was to reveal to this people what the Lord has revealed to me, there is not a man or woman would stay with me."

39. Brigham Young, statement dated 8 Jan. 1845, in *Utah Genealogical and Historical Magazine* 11:106–108. Young also briefly mentions here another conjecture about Joseph Smith—that Smith was a direct descendant of Jesus Christ through Mary Magdalene. Later in Utah, Young openly taught that Jesus was married, had many children, and practiced polygamy. See Ogden Kraut, *Jesus Was Married* (Dugway, UT: Pioneer Books, 1969).

40. See J. R. Eardley, *Gems of Inspiration* (San Francisco, 1899).

41. JD 1:51.

42. Ibid., 8:179.

10.
The Mormon Concept of a Mother in Heaven

Linda P. Wilcox

THE IDEA OF A MOTHER IN HEAVEN IS A SHADOWY AND ELUSIVE one floating around the edges of Mormon consciousness. Mormons who grow up singing "O My Father" are familiar with the concept of a heavenly mother, but few hear much else about her. She exists, apparently, but has not been very evident in Mormon meetings or writings, and little if any "theology" has been developed to elucidate her nature and characterize our relationship to her.

Although nearly all world religions have had female divinities and feminine symbolism, the God of western Judeo-Christian culture and scripture has been almost unremittingly masculine. Still, the idea of a heavenly mother or a female counterpart to the male Father-God is not unknown in Christianity. Recently discovered gnostic texts from the first century after Jesus Christ reveal doctrine teaching about a divine mother as well as father. In some texts God is conceived of as a dyad, both male and female. There is also a body of writings which identifies the divine mother as the Holy Spirit, the third member of the Trinity, which then becomes a family group — the Father, Mother, and Son.[1]

Christianity has also had the elevation of Mary in Catholicism. From first being the Mother of God, Mary eventually became the mother of everyone as she took on a mediating function and became a divine presence to whom prayers could be addressed. This feminization of the divine made possible some further theological developments such as the fourteenth-century thought of Dame

Julian of Norwich, who wrote about the motherhood as well as father-
hood of God and developed a symbolism of Christ as Mother.[2]

The nineteenth-century American milieu from which Mormonism sprang had some prototypes for a female deity as well. Ann
Lee had proclaimed herself as the feminine incarnation of the Messiah, as Christ had been the male incarnation — a necessary balance
in her system since she described a god which was both male and
female, father and mother. The Father-Mother God of the Shakers
and Christian Scientists included both sexes in a form of divine
androgyny, as in this prayer by Mary Baker Eddy: "Father-Mother
God/ Loving Me/ Guard me while I sleep/ Guide my little feet up to
Thee."[3]

By the end of the century Elizabeth Cady Stanton in her
Woman's Bible was explaining Genesis 1:26–28 ("And God said, Let us
make man in our image, after our likeness . . . ") as implying the
"simultaneous creation of both sexes, in the image of God. It is
evident from the language," she writes, "that the masculine and
feminine elements were equally represented" in the Godhead which
planned the peopling of the earth. To her, as in the gnostic texts, a
trinity of Father, Mother, and Son was more rational, and she called
for "the recognition by the rising generation of an ideal Heavenly
Mother, to whom their prayers should be addressed, as well as to a
Father."[4]

Half a century before Stanton, the Mormon religion had
begun to develop a doctrine of just such a heavenly mother — a glorified goddess, spouse to an actual heavenly father, and therefore the
literal mother of our spirits. While the need for a divine feminine
element in religion is perhaps universal, the form it took in Mormonism was particularly well suited to other aspects of Mormon
theology. The Mother in Heaven concept was a logical and natural
extension of a theology which posited both an anthropomorphic
god who had once been a man and the possibility of eternal procreation of spirit children.

The origins of the Heavenly Mother concept in Mormonism
are shadowy. The best known exposition is, of course, Eliza R. Snow's
poem, "O My Father," or — the title it was known by earlier — "Invoca-
tion, or the Eternal Father and Mother." When the poem was first
published in the *Times and Seasons* (15 Nov. 1845, p. 1039) it carried

the notation, "City of Joseph, Oct. 1845," but the actual date of composition is not known. It does not appear in Eliza's notebook/diary for the years 1842–44.[5]

Although President Wilford Woodruff gave Snow credit for originating the idea—"That hymn is a revelation, though it was given unto us by a woman"[6]—it is more likely that Joseph Smith was the first to expound the doctrine of a mother in heaven. Joseph F. Smith claimed that God revealed that principle ("that we have a mother as well as a father in heaven") to Joseph Smith; that Joseph Smith revealed it to Eliza Snow Smith, his plural wife; and that Eliza Snow was inspired, being a poet, to put it into verse.[7]

Other incidents tend to confirm this latter view. Susa Young Gates told of Joseph Smith's consoling Zina Diantha Huntington on the death of her mother in 1839 by telling her that not only would she know her mother again on the other side, but, "More than that, you will meet and become acquainted with your eternal Mother, the wife of your Father in Heaven." Susa went on to say that about this same time Eliza Snow "learned the same glorious truth from the same inspired lips" and was then moved to put this truth into verse.[8] Since Zina Huntington and Eliza were close friends as well, it was also a likely possibility that Zina might have spoken of this idea to Eliza. David McKay recorded that during a buggy ride on which he accompanied Eliza Snow, he asked her if the Lord had revealed the Mother in Heaven doctrine to her. She replied no, that "I got my inspiration from the Prophets teachings all that I was required to do was to use my Poetical gift and give that Eternal principal in Poetry."[9]

Women were not the only ones to have had some acquaintance with the idea of a mother in heaven during the lifetime of Joseph Smith. There is a third-hand account of an experience related by Zebedee Coltrin: "One day the Prophet Joseph asked him [Coltrin] and Sidney Rigdon to accompany him into the woods to pray. When they had reached a secluded spot Joseph laid down on his back and stretched out his arms. He told the brethren to lie one on each arm, and then shut their eyes. After they had prayed he told them to open their eyes. They did so and saw a brilliant light surrounding a pedestal which seemed to rest on the earth. They closed their eyes and again prayed. They then saw, on opening them, the

Father seated upon a throne; they prayed again and on looking saw the Mother also; after praying and looking the fourth time they saw the Savior added to the group."[10]

Church leaders of the nineteenth century, although they did not speak much about a mother in heaven, seemed to accept the idea as commonsensical, that for God to be a father implied the existence of a mother as well. Brigham Young said that God "created man, as we create our children; for there is no other process of creation in heaven, on the earth, in the earth, or under the earth, or in all the eternities, that is, that were, or that ever will be"[11] — an indirect reference to the necessity of a mother for the process of creation. He also quoted his counselor Heber C. Kimball's recollection of Joseph Smith's saying "that he would not worship a God who had not a Father; and I do not know that he would if he had not a mother; the one would be as absurd as the other."[12]

Apostle Erastus Snow also used indirect inference in explaining the logic of the Heavenly Mother concept. "Now, it is not said in so many words in the Scriptures, that we have a Mother in heaven as well as a Father," he admitted. "It is left for us to infer this from what we see and know of all living things in the earth including man. The male and female principle is united and both necessary to the accomplishment of the object of their being, and if this be not the case with our Father in heaven after whose image we are created, then it is an anomaly in nature. But to our minds the idea of a Father suggests that of a Mother."[13]

Snow's position was somewhat distinct from that of other Mormon leaders in that he described God as a unity of male and female elements, much like the Shakers' Father-Mother God: " 'What,' says one, 'do you mean we should understand that Deity consists of man and woman?' Most certainly I do. If I believe anything that god has ever said about himself, and anything pertaining to the creation and organization of man upon the earth, I must believe that Deity consists of man and woman . . . there can be no god except he is composed of the man and woman united, and there is not in all the eternities that exist, nor ever will be, a God in any other way. . . . There never was a God, and there never will be in all eternities, except they are made of these two component parts; a man a woman; the male and the female."[14] To Erastus Snow, God was not a male personage, with a heavenly mother being a second divine personage; both of them together constituted God.

This development of theology by means of inference and commonsense extension of ordinary earth-life experience continued into the twentieth century. In fact, it is the primary approach taken by most of those who have made mention of a mother in heaven. Bruce R. McConkie in *Mormon Doctrine* (Salt Lake City: Bookcraft, 1966), for example, says that "An exalted and glorified Man of Holiness (Moses 6:57) could not be a Father unless a Woman of like glory, perfection, and holiness was associated with him as a Mother. The begetting of children makes a man a father and a woman a mother whether we are dealing with man in his mortal or immortal state" (p. 516). And Hugh B. Brown, then a member of the First Presidency, noted in 1961 that "some have questioned our concept of a mother in heaven, but no home, no church, no heaven would be complete without a mother there."[15]

One reason why little theology was developed about a heavenly mother is that the scriptural basis for the doctrine was slim. But Joseph Fielding Smith noted that "the fact that there is no reference to a mother in heaven either in the Bible, Book of Mormon or Doctrine and Covenants, is not sufficient proof that no such thing as a mother did exist there."[16] One possible reason for this gap in the scriptures is offered by a twentieth-century seminary teacher: "Considering the way man has profaned the name of God, the Father, and His Son, Jesus Christ, is it any wonder that the name of our Mother in Heaven has been withheld, not to mention the fact that the mention of Her is practically nil in scripture?"[17]

In looking next at statements by church leaders in the twentieth century, I would like to concentrate briefly on three time periods: the first decade of the century, the 1920s and 1930s, and finally the more recent decades of the 1960s and 1970s. I would also like to take note of some themes which are apparent in these time periods — themes which may illustrate developments in the larger society as well.

For example, immediately after the turn of the century one noticeable thread which ran through several comments about the Mother in Heaven was an association of that doctrine with the movement for women's rights, a major issue in the last years of the

nineteenth century, especially in Utah. James E. Talmage in discussing the status and mission of women spoke of the early granting of
the franchise to women in Utah and the Mormon church's claim that
woman is man's equal. In this context he then went on to say, "The
Church is bold enough to go so far as to declare that man has an
Eternal Mother in the Heavens as well as an Eternal Father, and in
the same sense 'we look upon woman as a being, essential in every
particular to the carrying out of God's purposes in respect to
mankind.'"[18] An article in the *Deseret News* (4 Feb. 1905) noted that
the truthfulness of the doctrine of a mother in heaven would eventually be accepted by the world—that "it is a truth from which, when
fully realized, the perfect 'emancipation' and ennobling of woman
will result." To many, the concept of a mother in heaven was a fitting
expression of a larger movement which aimed at raising the status of
women and expanding their rights and opportunities.

Another theme, evident elsewhere in American thought as
well as in Mormonism, was the yearning for a female divinity—the
need for a nurturing presence in the universe. A mother in heaven
thus exemplified and embodied all those maternal qualities which
men had experienced as so warm and soul-filling in their own mothers (or which they perhaps had not experienced and so now desper-
ately wanted) and which were generally absent in a male god that
perhaps reflected a stern, closed-in image of Victorian manhood. A
national article excerpted in the *Deseret News* (4 Feb. 1905) said that
the world was coming to accept the idea of a mother in heaven. It
spoke of the tendency for human beings to crave, especially in times
of grief and anguish, the tenderness, gentleness, and sympathy of a
mother-figure which must in some way "be resident in the Divine
Being." And in the *Latter-day Saints' Millennial Star* an article noted
how not only small children but also adults need and want a mother
figure as a divine personage: "The heart of man craves his faith and
has from time immemorial demanded the deification of woman."[19]

But also in that first decade of the twentieth century, in
1907, the Mormon church's teaching of the Mother in Heaven doctrine was criticized and challenged by the Salt Lake Ministerial
Association as being unchristian.[20] B. H. Roberts, one of the members of the church's Council of the Seventy, responded by claiming
that the ministers were inconsistent. They objected to the idea of
Jesus having a literal Heavenly Father, he said, but then they also

complained because "we believe that we have for our spirits a heavenly mother as well as a heavenly father! Now observe the peculiar position of these critics: It is all right for Jesus to have a mother; but it is all wrong for him to have a father. On the other hand, it is all right for men's spirits to have a Father in heaven, but our reviewers object to our doctrine of their having a mother there."[21]

Two years later the First Presidency of the Mormon church issued a statement entitled "The Origin of Man." Although much of this message was concerned with explicating a Mormon view of man's (and woman's) earthly origins, the statement also took up the question of man's (and woman's) spiritual beginnings as well. While couching the doctrine partially in abstract generalities such as that "man, as a spirit, was begotten and born of heavenly parents," the statement also made a clear and explicit reference to a mother in heaven. "All men and women are in the similitude of the universal Father and Mother," it said, "and are literally the sons and daughters of Deity."[22] By 1909, then, if not before, the Mother in Heaven doctrine was an official part of Mormon belief. Apostle Joseph Fielding Smith later described this as one of (presumably several) "official and authoritative statements" about this doctrine.[23]

In the 1920s and 1930s there seemed to be an emphasis on the idea of "eternal" or "everlasting" motherhood, with several sermons or articles having titles of this sort or dealing with this theme. Somehow it seemed important to emphasize that motherhood was as ongoing and eternal as was godhood. John A. Widtsoe, for example, found a "radiant warmth" in the "thought that among the exalted beings in the world to come we shall find a mother who possesses the attributes of Godhood. Such conceptions raise motherhood to a high position. They explain the generous provision made for women in the Church of Christ. To be a mother is to engage in the eternal work of God."[24]

Widtsoe's colleague Melvin J. Ballard carried on the theme of everlasting motherhood when he noted that "motherhood is eternal with Godhood, and there is no such thing as eternal or endless life without the eternal and endless continuation of motherhood." With more fervor than accuracy, Ballard claimed that there was not one single life form on earth without a mother—hence "there is no life in the realms that are above and beyond us, unless there also is a mother." Perhaps unaware of other strains of Christian thought—

not to mention other cultures and religions which worshiped female deities — Ballard called the Mother in Heaven concept a "startling doctrine" which was "so far as I know, never taught before in the history of the world." He also emphasized the noble, goddesslike aspects of the Heavenly Mother. She stands side by side with the Heavenly Father "in all her glory, a glory like unto his . . . a companion, the Mother of his children." She is "a glorified, exalted, ennobled Mother."[25]

German Ellsworth, who served as president of the church's Northern States Mission, also stressed the theme of "Eternal Motherhood," noting that finally, after eighty years, the world was coming to accept the doctrine that if we had a heavenly father we must have had a heavenly mother as well. Ellsworth linked this doctrine specifically to the "true mission of women" on the earth, which was to be mothers. In particular, "the women of Zion can rejoice and take heart in the great calling given to them, in being privileged to be the earthly mothers of the elect sons of our Heavenly Father." The Mother in Heaven concept seemed important to Ellsworth mainly as a role model for women to become mothers and to seek "to build up a better race — to successfully do their part in peopling the earth with a noble and intelligent class of citizens."[26] These examples share an attempt to raise the status of the mothering role, or of women specifically as mothers, by pointing out that the Mother in Heaven role is as important and eternal as that of God.

In more recent times we can see some widening out, with a greater variety of images presented by General Authorities who speak about a mother in heaven. Joseph Fielding Smith, much like Elizabeth Cady Stanton, quotes Genesis 1:26 — "Let *us* make man in our image after *our* likeness" (his italics) — and suggests, "Is it not feasible to believe that female spirits were created in the image of a 'Mother in Heaven'?"[27] His emphasis implies that a female goddess was involved in the planning and decision making, was part of whatever group of exalted beings decided to create earthly men and women.

H. Burke Peterson in 1974 emphasized the Heavenly Mother's role as producer of spirit offspring. In asking church members to count the cost of a mother working outside the home, he warned about the danger of becoming "a mother whose energy is so sapped that she is sometimes neglecting her call from the Lord, a call that will one day prepare her to become an eternal mother—a co-creator of spiritual offspring."[28] One supposes that by "her call" Peterson means the care of her children and is suggesting that the complex responsibility of nurturing and guiding one's children is the most valuable preparation for eventually becoming an exalted goddess-mother.

Four years later, President Spencer W. Kimball expressed a view of the Mother in Heaven as "the ultimate in maternal modesty" and "restrained, queenly elegance." He also emphasized her great influence on us: "Knowing how profoundly our mortal mothers have shaped us here," he said, "do we suppose her influence on us as individuals to be less if we live so as to return there?"[29] Here we have maternal nurturing attributes and also a recognition of an exalted goddess quality in the Mother in Heaven.

At the same General Conference Elder Neal A. Maxwell presented this version of the role and activities of our Heavenly Mother: "When we return to our real home, it will be with the 'mutual approbation' of those who reign in the 'royal courts on high.' There we will find beauty such as mortal 'eye hath not seen;' we will hear sounds of surpassing music which mortal 'ear hath not heard.' Could such a regal homecoming be possible without the anticipatory arrangements of a Heavenly Mother?"[30] One of a Heavenly Mother's duties, it seems, might be to provide an aesthetically pleasing environment with sights and sounds of unimaginable glory to welcome her children home.

"We honor woman when we acknowledge Godhood in her eternal Prototype," reported a 1910 article in the *Latter-day Saints' Millennial Star*.[31] This survey of some of the images which have been expressed about a less-than-well-defined entity suggest that one's concept of a mother in heaven may reflect one's views about real women and their roles. Those who see women as basically producers of babies might tend to emphasize the feminine deity's role as producer of spirit children. Those who consider women to be more refined and spiritual than men might emphasize the Heavenly Mother's nobility and queenly attributes—and so forth. Mother in Heaven can be almost whatever an individual Mormon envisions her to be. Perhaps, ironically, we thus set her up, despite herself, to fill the most basic maternal role of all—that of meeting the deepest needs of her children, whatever they might be.

— NOTES —

1. See Elaine H. Pagels, "What Became of God the Mother? Conflicting Images of God in Early Christianity," *Signs* (Winter 1976): 293–303.

2. See "Dame Julian of Norwich and Margery Kempe: Divine Motherhood and Human Sisterhood," in Elizabeth Clark and Herbert Richardson, *Women and Religion: A Feminist Sourcebook of Christian Thought* (New York: Harper & Row, 1977), 102–112.

3. Clark and Richardson, 164.

4. Ibid., 218.

5. Maureen Ursenbach Beecher, "The Eliza Enigma: The Life and Legend of Eliza R. Snow," *Charles Redd Monographs on Western History* 6 (Provo, UT: Brigham Young University Press, 1976), 34.

6. Wilford Woodruff, "Discourse," *Latter-day Saints' Millennial Star* 56 (April 1894): 229; hereafter *Millennial Star*.

7. Joseph F. Smith, "Discourse," *Deseret Evening News*, 9 Feb. 1895. I am indebted to Maureen Ursenbach Beecher for much of this information.

8. Susa Young Gates, *History of the Young Ladies' Mutual Improvement Association* (Salt Lake City: Deseret News, 1911), 15–16.

9. David McKay to Mrs. James Hood, 16 March 1916, photocopy of holograph in possession of Maureen Ursenbach Beecher, courtesy of Shirley Bailey.

10. Abraham H. Cannon Journal, 25 Aug. 1880, archives, Historical Department, Church of Jesus Christ of Latter-day Saints, Salt Lake City, Utah; hereafter church archives.

11. Brigham Young, et al., *Journal of Discourses*, 26 vols. (Liverpool: Latter-day Saints' Book Depot, 1855–86), 11:122; hereafter JD.

12. JD 9:286.

13. JD 26:214.

14. JD 19:269–70.

15. Hugh B. Brown, "Relief Society—An Extension of the Home," *Relief Society Magazine* 48 (Dec. 1961): 814.

16. Joseph Fielding Smith, *Answers to Gospel Questions* (Salt Lake City: Deseret Book, 1960), 3:142.

17. Melvin R. Brooks, *LDS Reference Encyclopedia* (Salt Lake City: Bookcraft, 1960), 309–10.

18. *Deseret News*, 28 April 1902.

19. "Our Mother in Heaven," *Millennial Star* 72 (29 Sept. 1910): 619.

20. *Salt Lake Herald*, 4 June 1907, 8.

21. B. H. Roberts, "Answer to Ministerial Association Review," 9 June 1907 (Salt Lake City, 1907), 18–19.

22. First Presidency, "The Origin of Man," *Improvement Era* 13 (Nov. 1909): 80.

23. Joseph Fielding Smith, "Mothers in Israel," *Relief Society Magazine* 57 (Dec. 1970): 884.

24. John A. Widtsoe, "Everlasting Motherhood," *Millennial Star* 90 (10 May 1928): 298.

25. Melvin J. Ballard, address, 8 May 1921, in Journal History, under date, church archives.

26. German E. Ellsworth, "Eternal Motherhood," *Deseret News*, 7 May 1932.

27. Smith, *Answers to Gospel Questions*, 144.

28. H. Burke Peterson, address, *Ensign* 4 (May 1974): 32.

29. Spencer W. Kimball, address, *Ensign* 8 (May 1978): 11.

30. Neal A. Maxwell, address, *Ensign* 8 (May 1978): 11.

31. "Our Mother in Heaven," 620.

11.
The Origin of the Human Spirit in Early Mormon Thought

Van Hale

"WHERE DID WE COME FROM?" IS THE FIRST OF THREE QUESTIONS
familiar to Mormons today, thanks to the official missionary lessons
and other texts. The response—that we came from a premortal existence where our spirits were literally begotten by a heavenly father
and a heavenly mother—is a doctrine most Mormons accept. It has
been taught in sermons, articles, books, and manuals from the
church's beginning. Closely related is the belief that the resurrected
faithful of this earth will do what God has been doing: procreate
spirit children for future worlds. Few, if any, teachings are more
widely believed among Mormons, but the origin of the preexistence
doctrine has remained somewhat obscure.

Although there are no clear statements of the doctrine in
any of the church's four standard works, Mormons sometimes cite
several New Testament passages in support. For example, Hebrews
12:9 speaks of God as the "Father of spirits"; in Acts 17:28, Paul calls
men the "offspring" of God; and in Galatians 4 and Romans 8, Paul
calls certain men "sons of God." But these passages do not state that
God procreated our spirits, and while a premortal spirit birth may
be inferred by the terms "Father," "sons," and "offspring," the more
likely intent of these biblical authors is that God is the father of those
who accept the gospel and are adopted as his spiritual children.
Even if it could be argued persuasively that the authors believed in a

premortal spirit birth, this would be a unique interpretation un-known to previous biblical scholars, and the question would still remain, When in Mormonism and by whom did this interpretation originate?

In Mormon scripture the one passage used to support the spirit birth doctrine is Doctrine and Covenants 76:24 in which the inhabitants of the different worlds are referred to as "begotten sons and daughters unto God." However, the context of this passage is that the inhabitants of the worlds are begotten sons and daughters unto God through Jesus Christ. The reference to sons and daughters clearly means "adopted" spiritual children — not spirit children — and does not refer to the idea of literal procreation by God. The doctrine clearly did not originate in scripture. This should not be surprising since most LDS scripture was produced while Mormon theology was in its infancy, and there is little in LDS canon from the theologically productive Nauvoo, Illinois, period of the early to mid-1840s.

In tracing the doctrine of spirit birth backwards we find hundreds of references to it throughout Mormon literature, and the teaching that spirits originated through premortal procreation seems to have been the prevailing explanation ever since the Nauvoo period. What is surprising, however, is that none of Joseph Smith's recorded sermons — including those delivered in Nauvoo — teach the doctrine. In fact, several seem to teach a doctrine logically at odds with the belief that spirits are the literal offspring of God through premortal birth.

While two references to the spirit birth doctrine were writ-ten by Mormons during Joseph Smith's lifetime, Smith's own doctri-nal teaching was that the human spirit as a conscious entity is eter-nal — as eternal as God. It has no beginning and has no end. It was not created; it is self-existing. God, being more advanced than the other spirits, organized them and instituted laws to give them the privilege to advance like himself. He presides and will preside over them throughout eternity. Smith used the terms "spirit," "soul," "intelligence," and "mind" synonymously to describe the inchoate, indestructible essence of life.

This summary is drawn from eight documentary sources — dating from 6 May 1833 to 7 April 1844. None of them suggest that God presides over the spirits because they are his begotten offspring, but because he was more intelligent, more advanced, than they and because he organized them into a premortal council.

The earliest reference to the uncreated, eternal portion of all human beings is from the Doctrine and Covenants 93:29, dated 6 May 1833: "Man was also in the beginning with God. Intelligence, or the light of truth, was not created or made, neither indeed can be." This statement, although brief to the point of being ambiguous, does indicate that *some* aspect of individual existence was not created.

The date of the second statement, recorded by Apostle Willard Richards, is uncertain but undoubtedly occurred during the years 1839–1841. Here the spirit is not created and the "Father" is referred to as "organizer": "The Spirit of Man is not a created being; it existed from Eternity & will exist to eternity. Anything created cannot be Eternal. . . . The Father called all spirits before him at the creation of Man & organized them. He (Adam) is the head, was told to multiply."[1]

The next statement, from a sermon Smith delivered in Washington, D.C., on 6 February 1840, was published in an eastern newspaper. Note here that "soul" is synonymous with "spirit" and is without beginning: "I believe that God is eternal. That He had no beginning, and can have no end. Eternity means that which is without beginning or end. I believe that the *soul* is eternal; and had no beginning; it can have no end. . . . the soul of man, the spirit, had existed from eternity in the bosom of Divinity."[2]

The following is from another of Smith's discourses, this one delivered to a school of instruction at Nauvoo on 5 January 1841. Note again that "soul" seems to be synonymous with "spirit," that it has no beginning, and that spirits were *organized* in the preexistence: "If the soul of man had a beginning it will surely have an end. . . . Spirits are eternal. At the first organization in heaven we were all present and saw the Savior chosen and appointed, and the plan of salvation made and we sanctioned it."[3]

Fifth is a 28 March 1841 statement Smith made to the school at Nauvoo. Again, "spirit" seems to be synonymous with "intelligence," it is self existent, God was a superior intelligence, and God organized a premortal council: "the spirit or the inteligence of men are self Existant principles before the foundation [of] this Earth . . . God saw that those intelegences had Not power to Defend themselves against those that had a tabernicle therefore the Lord Calls them togather in Counsel & agrees to form them tabernicles."[4]

The next documentary source is composed of parts of three verses from the "Book of Abraham" (3:18, 22–23), published at Nauvoo in 1842. Again spirits have no beginning; the terms "spirit," "intelligence," and "soul" are used interchangeably; and God organized the spirits into a premortal council: "18.... if there be two spirits, and one shall be more intelligent than the other, yet these two spirits, notwithstanding one is more intelligent than the other, have no beginning; they existed before, they shall have no end, they shall exist after, for they are gnolaum, or eternal. 22. Now the Lord had shown unto me, Abraham, the intelligences that were organized before the world was; and among all these there were many of the noble and great ones; 23. And God saw these souls that they were good, and he stood in the midst of them, and he said: These I will make my rulers; for he stood among those that were spirits ... "

In 1845 George Laub was writing his journal from memory and using scraps of notes he had taken from 1843 and 1844. The following comes from his report of a Smith sermon which Laub dates 6 April 1843: "How came Spirits? Why, they are and ware Self Existing as all eternity & our Spirits are as Eternal as the very God is himself & that we choose to come on this Earth to take unto ourselvs tabernakles by permition of our Father."[5]

The last, and most extensive, statement of Joseph Smith is from his so-called King Follett discourse, delivered at a General Conference of the church on 7 April 1844. The address eulogized King Follett, who had recently died, and reassured friends and family of the eternal nature of individual existence. Four reports of this discourse were recorded: one by Thomas Bullock and one by William Clayton, both of whom were officially appointed clerks or reporters of the conference; one by Willard Richards, who was keeping Joseph Smith's diary; and one by Apostle Wilford Woodruff for his own diary. In 1855 these four reports were amalgamated into the version found in current editions of the official *History of the Church*, which, I believe, allows for an interpretation not intended by Joseph Smith.

The following quotation, which I believe more closely represents the thinking of Joseph Smith, is taken from Bullock's and Clayton's versions.[6] Note again that spirit has no beginning—it was

not created; that "spirit," "mind," "soul," and "intelligence" are synonymous; and that God, being greater than the other spirits, instituted laws so that the spirits could advance like himself: " . . . the soul,
the mind of man, the immortal spirit. All men say God created it in
the beginning. The very idea lessens man in my estimation; I do not
believe the doctrine . . . The mind of man is as immortal as God
himself. I know that my testimony is true, hence when I talk to these
mourners; what have they lost, they are only separated from their
bodies for a short season; their spirits existed coequal with God, and
they now exist in a place where they converse together, the same as
we do on the earth. It is [not] logic to say that a spirit is immortal, and
yet have a beginning. Because if a spirit have a beginning it will have
an end; [not] good logic. . . . I take my ring from my finger and liken
it unto the mind of man, the immortal spirit, because it has no
beginning. . . . All the fools, learned and wise men, from the beginning of creation, who say that man had a beginning, proves that he
must have an end and then the doctrine of annihilation would be
true. But, if I am right I might with boldness proclaim from the
house tops, that God never did have power to create the spirit of man
at all. God himself could not create himself: intelligence exists upon
a self existent principle, it is a spirit from age to age, and, there is no
creation about it. . . . God himself finds himself in the midst of spirits
and glory, because he was greater, and because he saw proper to
institute laws, whereby the rest could have a privilege to advance like
himself, that they might have one glory upon another, in all that
knowledge, power, and glory, &c., in order to save the world of
spirits."[7]

Although Smith seems not to have taught that spirits come
into existence through a birth process, apostles Lorenzo Snow and
Orson Pratt believed such a doctrine during Smith's lifetime. On 14
February 1842, Snow, at the time a missionary in England, wrote the
following to an Elder Walker: "When I write to you I feel to let my
imagination rove I do not know why may be because you are sometimes as foolish as myself wish to know and dwell upon *big things* of
the kingdom.

"Then let us indulge our follies at this time and wander a
moment into the field of imagination. Some thirteen thousand years
ago in Heaven or in Paradise (say) we came into existence or in other
words received a spiritual organization according to the laws that

govern spiritual births in eternity We were there and then (say) born in the express image and likeness of him by whom we received our spiritual birth possessing the same faculties & powers but in their infantile state yet susceptable of an elevation equal to that of those possessed by our Spiritual Father But in order to effect this we must needs be planted in a material tabernacle. Accordingly the great machine was set in motion whereby bodies for the immortal sons and daughters of God came into being ... the sons of God or the spirits awaiting to be perfected shouted with joy in anticipation of one day being like their Father in all things both in relation to becoming the Father of Spirits and that of Glorified bodies."[8]

When Pratt wrote about this doctrine, he chose not to relegate it to the realm of speculative "imagination," publishing it under the heading "The Mormon Creed" in his *Prophetic Almanac for 1845*. Pratt wrote the pamphlet while in Washington, D.C., in the spring of 1844, just prior to Smith's death.[9] Brigham Young endorsed Pratt's work at the October 1844 General Conference.[10] In it Pratt presents the following catechism: "What is man? The offspring of God. What is God? The father of man. Who is Jesus Christ? He is our brother. . . . How many states of existence has man? He has three. What is the first? It is spiritual. What is the second? It is temporal. What is the third? It is immortal and eternal. How did he begin to exist in the first? He was begotten and born of God. How did he begin to exist in the second? He was begotten and born of the flesh."[11]

In addition, articles on the spirit birth doctrine, authored by several of Joseph Smith's close associates, appeared in the church's official organ, the *Times and Seasons*, shortly after his death. In one article, published in February 1845, Apostle John Taylor wrote: "that Jesus Christ had a father and mother of his Spirit, and a father and mother of his flesh; and so have all of his brethren and sisters . . . "[12] Issues the following May and June published a story by William W. Phelps entitled "Paracletes." One of the important points of the story is that premortal spirits are the offspring of a father and mother and would "be born of the flesh as they had been of the spirit."[13] In the June issue the spirit birth doctrine was again published in Apostle Orson Pratt's address at the funeral of William Smith's wife, Caroline.[14] And in the November issue Joseph Smith's plural wife Eliza R. Snow published her poem "My Father in

Heaven" (better known today as "O My Father"). Snow's poem is dated October 1845 and speaks of a mother in heaven and of a spirit birth and childhood. Snow indicates that these concepts were unknown to her until Mormonism provided the "key of knowledge."[15]

Joseph Smith was without question *the* doctrinal authority among the Mormons. Baptism for the dead, eternal marriage, plural marriage, the nature of God, the plurality of gods, and men becoming gods are some of the concepts promulgated by the Saints after they were taught by Joseph Smith. During the months preceding Smith's death in June 1844, his teachings were questioned by some and rejected by others. In the succession crisis following his death one of the main issues was whether to carry on with *all* of his doctrines. The Twelve Apostles and their followers were dedicated disciples, determined to perpetuate what Smith had begun. It was in this setting that Taylor, Pratt, Phelps, and Snow publicly taught the spirit birth doctrine unaware or unconcerned that they might be contradicting Smith's doctrine. While the origin of spirits was not one of the controversial doctrines debated at the time, one would nonetheless not expect Smith's faithful followers to teach a doctrine that did not originate with him.

Another factor in determining the origin of this teaching involves the doctrine of eternal marriage. There is no doubt that Smith taught that one of the purposes of polygamy was eternal procreation. In his autobiography Apostle Parley P. Pratt recalls spending several days with Smith in Philadelphia in 1840. Pratt says that he was taught for the first time "of eternal family organization, and the eternal union of the sexes" resulting in "an offspring as numerous as the stars of heaven, or the sands of the sea shore."[16] Three years later, on 16 May 1843, William Clayton recorded that Smith taught privately, "Except a man and his wife enter into an everlasting covenant and be married for eternity, while in this probation, by the power and authority of the Holy Priesthood, they will cease to increase when they die; that is, they will not have any children after the resurrection. But those who are married by the power and authority of the priesthood in this life, and continue without committing the sin against the Holy Ghost will continue to increase and have children in the celestial glory."[17]

Two months later Smith dictated Doctrine and Covenants

132 in which those married for eternity are promised "a continuation of the seeds forever and ever. Then shall they be gods" (vv.
19–20). Here Smith implies that gods procreate but does not specify
that their offspring are spirits. There is no known explanation from
Smith on this subject. In a 16 July 1843 sermon he explained "that he
could not reveal the fulness of these things untill the Temple is
completed,"[18] which was not accomplished until after his death.
However, the conclusion some of his contemporaries drew, and the
one which has prevailed through Mormon history, is that children
born after the resurrection to exalted couples will be spirit children
for future worlds.

As far as I know, only one statement of Joseph Smith can be
interpreted to suggest that he believed in this particular doctrine of
spirit birth. It is found in a brief sketch of a sermon delivered on 16
July 1843, recorded by Franklin D. Richards. He reports Smith teaching that "Those who keep no eternal Law in this life or make no
eternal contract are single & alone in the eternal world . . . [it] is by
the multiplication of Lives that the eternal worlds are created and
occupied that which is born of the flesh is flesh that which is born of
the Spirit is Spirit."[19] In a note following his report Richards concludes: "From the above I deduce that we may make an eternal
covenant with our wives and in the resurrection claim that which is
our own and enjoy blessings & glories peculiar to those in that
condition even the multiplication of spirits in the eternal world."[20]
The prophet's point is sufficiently unclear to force Richards to deduce his meaning, and Richards's interpretation is not, by any
means, the only interpretation. William Clayton recorded a brief
synopsis of the sermon, but he did not include the statement on the
"multiplication of Lives."

Thus, while it seems certain that Smith taught that gods
procreate, he did not specify that their offspring are necessarily
spirits. And it is equally unclear if the alternative possibility, that the
offspring of the gods are physical children, would be any more
plausible in the prophet's thinking.

The difficulty of harmonizing Joseph Smith's teaching that
spirits have no beginning with the contemporary Mormon belief
that spirits come into existence through a spirit birth has been
resolved in two different ways.[21] According to one view, it is not the
spirit which is uncreated but "unorganized spirit matter," and

through the process of spirit birth to heavenly parents this uncreated spirit matter is formed into a conscious spirit being. Thus man's spirit is as eternal as any other physical object, since the *elements* of both are eternal. But because the spirit is a conscious being with a beginning to its existence, Joseph Smith might argue that the spirit can also cease to exist, that it can be destroyed and returned to its original state. Brigham Young, in fact, taught that those who do not progress will "regress" until they are disorganized and return to their native element. While this may harmonize the idea that spirit is eternal with the idea that spirits come into being through a spirit birth, it is foreign to Joseph Smith's doctrinal statements. Smith's interchangeable use of uncreated "mind," "soul," "intelligence," and "spirit," as well as his description in the King Follett discourse of spirits communicating, portray spirits as beings. When he declared that spirits are eternal, he was clearly speaking of beings, not of uncreated inanimate spirit matter.

According to the second view, the spirit was born of heavenly parents. It is the mind or intelligence which is without beginning. Through procreation a spirit body is created to clothe the uncreated intelligence. The leading proponent of this theory was B. H. Roberts.[22] Although this view—that an conscious entity, not inanimate matter, is uncreated—is closer to Joseph Smith's own teaching, Roberts relied on the textually inferior 1855 amalgamation of the King Follett discourse. In the earlier 1844 version, "mind," "intelligence," "soul," and "spirit" are used synonymously and are declared to be eternal, uncreated, and without beginning. But in the 1855 version, the mind or intelligence is only *part* of the spirit—the immortal part. This allows for the belief in a procreated spirit clothing the uncreated mind or intelligence. These later modifications were made eleven years after the discourse and are not supported by any of the four original reports.

Roberts thought Joseph Smith taught that the "intelligence *of* spirits" is uncreated, while the best evidence holds that Smith taught that the "intelligence *or* spirit" is uncreated. Others who believed like Roberts include John A. Widtsoe, James E. Talmage, and Joseph Fielding Smith.[23] While this teaching is closer to Smith's belief and represents the interpretation which will probably endure in Mormonism, I do not believe that it represents the doctrine of Joseph Smith on the topic.

After arriving in Utah in 1847, Brigham Young taught on a number of occasions that God is both the literal father of our spirits and the progenitor of our flesh and that those who are exalted will beget both physical and spirit children. According to Young, the first physical bodies born on each world are the offspring of the god of that world.[24] Although I have found no statement of Joseph Smith that either God or exalted men will beget physical children, Smith did teach that everything comes through a progenitor. For example, on 16 June 1844, he said publicly, "Where was there ever a son without a father? And where was there ever a father without first being a son? Whenever did a tree or anything spring into existence without a progenitor? And everything comes in this way."[25] This suggests that the first physical beings on this earth were begotten. If Smith believed that the offspring of God are physical beings, not spirits, then there would be no conflict between the belief that spirits have no beginning and the belief that gods procreate. The spirit birth would, according to this view, be an expansion based on a misunderstanding of Smith's ambiguous pronouncements.

Based on a careful reading of the documentary sources, it seems clear that Smith taught the doctrine that God organized a group of eternal spirits who were less advanced than he. To enable them to progress as he had done, he organized the earth. He came here with his wife and, by begetting the first physical children him-self, began the process which now provides physical bodies for the spirits he formerly organized. Those from this earth who gain exal-tation will do likewise. While this view harmonizes Smith's state-ments, it has two weaknesses. First, there is no explicit statement in support of this view from Joseph Smith. Second, none of his close associates taught it; in fact, I have found *no* Mormon who has ever advocated it, even though it seems to be the most plausible explana-tion of Smith's meaning.

In conclusion, one of the cherished doctrines of Mormon-ism, that spirits are the literal offspring of God, has been taught by virtually all Mormon leaders. The notable exception is probably Joseph Smith, whose direct statements teach a doctrine contrary to that of his closest associates, men and women who maintain that they were simply perpetuating what he had begun. Either the Mormon spirit birth doctrine was the result of Smith's early followers mis-understanding the prophet's doctrinal statements, or they taught unrecorded doctrine taught by Smith privately in Nauvoo, however much in conflict with Smith's earlier teachings.

— NOTES —

1. In Andrew F. Ehat and Lyndon W. Cook, *The Words of Joseph Smith* (Provo, UT: Religious Studies Center, Brigham Young University, 1980), 9.

2. Ibid., 33, 46–47. The original newspaper has not yet been located.

3. Ibid., 60.

4. Ibid., 68.

5. In Eugene England, ed., "George Laub's Nauvoo Journal," *Brigham Young University Studies* 18 (Winter 1978): 171–72. England argues in a footnote that Laub's dating of the sermon is in error and that it is probably Laub's report of Joseph Smith's King Follett discourse, given on 7 April 1844.

6. The four reports, the 1844 amalgamation, and the 1855 amalgamation are discussed in my "The King Follett Discourse: Textual History and Criticism," *Sunstone* 8 (Sept./Oct. 1983): 5–12.

7. *Times and Seasons* 5 (15 Aug. 1844): 615.

8. From a letter dated 14 Feb. 1842, in Lorenzo Snow Notebook, typescript, 75–76, archives, Church of Jesus Christ of Latter-day Saints, Salt Lake City.

9. See *Latter-day Saints' Millennial Star* 27:88.

10. See *Times and Seasons* 5 (1 Nov. 1844): 693.

11. Orson Pratt, *Prophetic Almanac for 1845*, n.p.

12. "The Living God," *Times and Seasons* 6 (15 Feb. 1845): 808–809.

13. "Paracletes," *Times and Seasons* 6 (1 May 1845): 891–92. Phelps included the idea of a mother in heaven in the song, "A Voice from the Prophet, 'Come to Me,'" which he wrote for the dedication of the Seventies' Hall at Nauvoo in December 1844. See *Times and Seasons* 6 (15 Jan. 1845): 783.

14. *Times and Seasons* 6 (1 June 1845): 920.

15. Eliza R. Snow, "My Father in Heaven," *Times and Seasons* 6 (15 Nov. 1845): 1,039.

16. Parley P. Pratt, ed., *Autobiography of Parley P. Pratt* (Salt Lake City: Deseret Book, 1966), 297–98.

17. In *History of the Church*, B. H. Roberts, ed., 7 vols. (Salt Lake City: Deseret Book, 1965), 5:391.

18. Ehat and Cook, 233.

19. Ibid., 232.

20. Ibid., 293.

21. See Blake Ostler, "The Idea of the Pre-existence in the Development of Mormon Thought," *Dialogue: A Journal of Mormon Thought* 15 (Spring 1982): 63–74.

22. See ibid., 68–72.

23. See ibid., 69–72.

24. For Brigham Young's teachings, see *Journal of Discourses*, 26 vols. (Liverpool: Latter-day Saints Booksellers Depot, 1855–86), 4:218; 6:275; and *Deseret News*, 18 Sept. 1852.

25. *History of the Church*, 5:476.

12.
The Idea of Preexistence in Mormon Thought

Blake T. Ostler

MOST MORMONS ASSUME THAT A DOCTRINE OF PREEXISTENCE has always characterized their theology. However, the teaching encountered by the earliest Mormons did not depart significantly from the prevailing Christian view of a single, infinite, and absolute God who created everything from nothing. Although a doctrine of the preexistence of human souls was accepted by Origen, the brilliant second-century theologian, it was officially condemned in 543 A.D. Catholic doctrine more typically vacillated bétween the view that all persons existed seminally in Adam (a view known as traducianism) and the view that all persons are created "from nothing" at the moment of conception.[1] (Angels and demons were usually thought to be products of a separate creation and were unrelated to humans.)

The earliest Mormon publications defined God—in terms borrowed from contemporary orthodox Christianity—as the sole and necessary basis of all existence.[2] The concept of a preexistence either in the sense of eternal, uncreated spirits co-existing with God or as spirit offspring of God did not exist in early Mormon thought. The Book of Mormon assumed that human existence depended entirely upon God (see, for example, Mos. 2:20–21). When the premortal Lord revealed his finger to the brother of Jared, he explained that humans were created "in the beginning after mine own image . . . after the body of my spirit" (Eth. 3:15–16), implying that human, physical bodies resemble God's spiritual body.[3] In contrast, orthodox Christianity interpreted "image and likeness" (Gen. 1:26)

to mean humankind's moral capacities, not its physical attributes.[4]
The seeds, at least, of anthropomorphism and of co-existence of
humans with God were thus planted in Mormon thought in the Book
of Mormon notion of creation after the image of God's spiritual
body.

   Some Mormons have understood Alma 13 to teach the preexistence of humans because it refers to an ordination "prepared
before the foundation of the world" (v. 3).[5] However, a close reading
suggests that the ordination was not based on actions made *prior* to
mortality but according to the foreknowledge of God (vv. 3, 7). This
notion is identical to the Arminian doctrine that God ordains people to salvation based on their good works foreseen by God and not
because of preexistence. That early Mormons did not see an idea of
preexistence explicitly taught in the Book of Mormon, and that the
earliest Mormon converts were unaware of the doctrine, is apparent
from Mormon apostle Orson Pratt's comment: "This same doctrine
[of premortal existence] is inculcated in some small degree in the
Book of Mormon. However, I do not think that I should have ever
discerned it in that book had it not been for the new translation of
[the Bible by Joseph Smith]."[6]

   The classical gulf between God and his mortal creations
entailed in the doctrine of *creatio ex nihilo* was accepted without
revision in the official Mormon publication *The Evening and the Morning Star* in October 1832: "The Creator, who having created our souls
at first by an act of his will can either eternally preserve them or
absolutely annihilate them" (p. 77). Humans were thus contingent
beings who did not exist prior to their creation by God—either as
body or as spirit—and could lapse into non-being if God willed it. A
letter in the May 1835 *Latter Day Saints' Messenger and Advocate* echoed
a similar belief: "Man is dependent on the great first cause and is
constantly upheld by Him, therefore justly amenable to him" (p.
113).

   Nevertheless, the Book of Mormon foreshadowed a kind of
preexistence by treating the Adamic myth as an expression of ge-
neric human experience. Book of Mormon prophet Alma explained
the necessity of the Atonement by noting that "mankind" had fallen
from God's presence and could "return" only through the Atonement (Al. 42:7, 14; see also 2 Ne. 2:21, 25; Al. 34:9; 41:9). The Book of
Mormon inculcated (to borrow Orson Pratt's term) the belief that

humanity existed in God's presence—at least, on a mythic level— prior to the Fall, and identified all humans with Adam in a corporate existence. If one were to identify a point from which the Mormon idea of preexistence developed, this description of humanity's fall from the presence of God would be, in my opinion, the best candidate.

Joseph Smith's 1830 commentary on Genesis, later published as the Book of Moses, marked the next development in the notion of a preexistence. Since at least the second century A.D., Christian writers recognized a contradiction between Genesis 1:26–27, which declares that man was created in the image and likeness of God, and Genesis 2:5, which declares that there was not yet a man to till the ground.[7] Numerous early Christian writers had tried to resolve the problem by treating Genesis 1:1–2:3 as a "conceptual blueprint" of God's plan to create the world and Genesis 2:4f as an account of the actual physical creation.[8] Joseph Smith expanded the Genesis text in his Book of Moses to provide a similar explanation: "4. [T]hese are the generations of the heaven and of the earth, when they were created, in the day that I, the Lord God, made the heaven and the earth, 5. And every plant of the field before it was on the earth, and every herb of the field before it grew. For I the Lord God, *created all things of which I have spoken, spiritually, before they were naturally upon the face of the earth. . . . And I, the Lord God, had created all the children of men*; and not yet a man to till the ground; *for in heaven created I them*; and there was not yet flesh upon the earth. . . . 7. And I, the Lord God, formed man from the dust . . . and man became a living soul . . . *nevertheless, all things were before created; but spiritually were they created and made according to my word. 9. And [every tree] also became a living soul. For it was spiritual in the day that I created it; for it remaineth in the sphere in which I, God, created it, yea, even all things which I prepared for the use of man"* (Moses 3:4–9; italics indicate text added by Joseph Smith).

Two possible explanations for what it means to be "created spiritually" before existing "naturally on the earth" can be ascertained from context. First, it should be noted that the term "spirit" was not clarified in Mormon usage until 1843 to mean "pure" or "refined" matter, and "to create" was not clarified until 1842 to mean to "organize" rather than creation out of nothing.[9] Prior to this, Mormon use of these terms was similar to the Christian definition of creation *ex nihilo*. Indeed, the fact that Smith, in the 1840s, corrected "to create" in Genesis to mean to organize rather than to create from nothing suggests that those to whom he spoke did not yet know or appreciate the difference. Further, the early nineteenth-century usage of the word "spiritual" often implied a conceptual or intellectual blueprint without connoting real (i.e., mind-independent) existence. Moses 3:7 indicated that the physical creation proceeded "according to [God's] word." That is, God formed the idea and spoke the command before the actions occurred. This is consistent with Smith's later redaction in the Book of Abraham. (See also Moses 6:61-63, which identifies God's plan of salvation as the spiritual likeness of temporal things).

On the other hand, the key to these passages may be the phrase, "for it remaineth in the sphere in which I God created it" (Moses 3:9). This phrase was also used in 2 Nephi 2:22-23 to describe the status of Adam in the Garden of Eden prior to the Fall: "if Adam had not transgressed he would have remained in the Garden of Eden. And all things which were created must have remained in the same state in which they were created." This may refer to an intermediate, paradisiacal existence unique to Adam and Eve. According to the Book of Mormon, only with the Fall did the temporal world, including a temporal Adam, come into existence. Thus, Adam existed spiritually *only* after being placed in the garden, and in mortality *only* after the Fall. The Book of Moses speaks of Adam being created in the beginning but placed in the Garden of Eden in a state of innocence prior to his existence in a mortal state. A popular nineteenth-century occult teaching involved a prototypic, androgynous Adam in a "spiritual body" before the Fall prior to the existence of "terrestrial man."[10] (This is another way of viewing the same transient state of being in the garden.)

This interpretation of the Book of Moses is supported by a revelation to Joseph Smith in September 1830 which he received while working on the Book of Moses. The revelation explained that "*the devil was before Adam*, for he rebelled against me saying, give me thine honor" (Book of Commandments, chap. 29) The story corresponding to Moses 4:1-4 is then recounted. The meaning of this revelation appears to be that in a pre-earth time, before Adam existed, Satan rebelled against God. The relation of this revelation to the Book of Moses and to the Book of Mormon seems clear: Adam did not exist until he was spiritually created in the Garden of Eden. The notion that everyone preexisted in the Garden of Eden in Adam is also reinforced by the Book of Moses' comment that Adam "is many" (1:34). This theme of identifying all humans in a corporate existence in Adam was adopted in the later temple endowment creation narrative.[11]

The next development in the Mormon concept of preexistence occurred in a May 1833 revelation that reinforced the idea of humankind existing in the beginning only as an aspect of God's intelligence or knowledge of all truth (i.e., "ideal" or mind-dependent existence): "Ye were also in the beginning with the Father: that which is Spirit, even the Spirit of Truth; and truth is knowledge of things as they are, and as they were, and as they are to come. . . . Man was also in the beginning with God. Intelligence, or the light of truth was not created or made, neither can it be. All truth is independent in that sphere in which god has placed it, to act for itself, as all intelligence also. . . . Every spirit of man was innocent in the beginning (D&C 1835, 82: 4–6; D&C 93 in current LDS editions).

This passage suggests that humanity preexisted "ideally" as part of God's knowledge of all things and was not independent of God's knowledge. That ideal preexistence was probably intended in this revelation is evident from two observations. First, "intelligence" is singular and defines God's knowledge and glory, and is not plural in the sense of self-existent individuals, as it would be in the later Book of Abraham. Second, in every instance where man is said to "exist in the beginning with the Father" (vv. 23, 29) the statement is clarified to mean that humans existed in God's knowledge of truth (vv. 23–24, 29).

Other passages in this revelation foreshadow *real* preexistence, or existence independent of God's mind. For example, the 1833 revelation states: "all truth is independent in that sphere in which God placed it, to act for itself, as all intelligence also, otherwise there is no existence" (v. 31). Mormonism did not yet have a notion of individualized human spirits, human intelligence being nothing more than an extension of God's uncreated spirit. In fact, as late as 1839 Apostle Parley P. Pratt wrote that when dry land and the Great Deep became "filled with the quickening, or life giving substance which we call spirit," they produced living creatures. When

the human form was infused with the same life force, it also "quickened him with life and animation." Pratt's view, which derived from
Joseph Smith's teachings, held that "it was not a personal spirit that
quickened the body, but rather an infused portion of the divine
spirit."[12] The notion that "man was also in the beginning with God"
and that "every spirit of man was innocent from the beginning" was
simply a confirmation that Adam was innocent when placed in the
Garden of Eden prior to mortal existence. However, the identification of individuals with Adam was actualized in the revelation so
that every individual human had the same moral qualities (i.e., innocence) as Adam prior to the Fall.

By 1835, however, Joseph Smith was developing the concept
of preexistence which he would later teach in Nauvoo, Illinois. In the
June 1835 *Messenger and Advocate* W. W. Phelps, one of the prophet's
closest associates, stated: "We shall by and by learn that we were with
God in another world before the foundation of the world, and had
our agency, in order that we may prepare ourselves for a kingdom of
glory" (p. 130). Phelps's statement is evidence that Joseph Smith was
probably reconsidering his teachings on man and God in light of the
developing doctrines of plurality of worlds and plurality of gods.
The following month Joseph Smith obtained the Egyptian papryi
from which he would produce the Book of Abraham, a document
confirming the individuality of spirits and preexistence. Phelps's
Messenger and Advocate statement is significant for at least three reasons: Phelps affirmed that people had agency in this "other world
before the foundation of [this] world"; implied that people existed
actually with God rather than ideally; and treated the doctrine of
preexistence as something new to his readers.

Other developments occurring in Mormon theology at this
time similarly affected the idea of preexistence. The Godhead, for
instance, was being differentiated into three separate personages;
the vision of the three degrees of glory (later D&C 76) suggested that
humans, like God, were ultimately uncreated; and reality—including spirit—was defined in materialistic terms. Previously spirit was
understood to be immaterial.[13]

By 1836 Joseph Smith had begun work on the Book of
Abraham, although it would not be published until 1842. In the
Book of Abraham, Joseph Smith expanded the discussion he had
begun in Moses 4:1-4 regarding the premortal council in which

Satan rebelled against God[14] and introduced the notion of "intelligences"—the individual, self-conscious, and autonomous essence of persons which existed from all eternity (see Abr. 3: 18, 22). Joseph Smith redefined the Hebrew term " 'olam" ("gnolaum" in the Book of Abraham)—which meant an indefinite period of time—to describe the nature of these spirits/intelligences to mean that they existed without beginning and without end. The unequal status of these spirits/intelligences meant that they were differentiated, not a single mass of spirit stuff. Further, they existed from all eternity. The Book of Abraham speaks of intelligences/spirits being "organized before the world was" (v. 22). However, "organization" did not mean organization of spirit body through spiritual birth, but social organization of the spirits into a heavenly council of preexisting entities.[15]

Joseph Smith did not distinguish between a time before which these spirits/intelligences were organized and a time after they were "born" as "spirit children"—in fact, the contemporary Mormon notion that God is the literal father of individual spirits through spirit birth would probably have been foreign to him. He taught that spirits were eternal and uncreated and used the terms "spirits" and "intelligences" synonymously. Joseph Smith's fullest statement of the doctrine of preexistence of humans was the King Follett discourse delivered shortly before his death in 1844. The prophet taught that human existence has the same ontological status as God's existence—that people cannot *not* exist, even in their spiritual essence. The theological significance of this fundamental departure from traditional Christian thought cannot be overstated.

Soon after Joseph Smith's death, however, the view that individual spirits existed without beginning would be modified by successors in favor of a concept of contingent preexistence more congenial to classical Christian absolutism. In this later development, only diffuse "spirit element" was considered uncreated; autonomous individual existence arose only after the organization of this eternal substance, or intelligence, into a spirit person through "spiritual birth." This concept was an outgrowth of the paradox between the doctrine popularized by Eliza R. Snow that individuals are literally begotten of divine parents and Smith's affirmation that humans, in an elementary state, are eternal. As a result, preexistence of individuals began with literal spiritual birth, while before this birth only unrefined and disorganized spirit, or intelligence, existed. "I will tell you how it is," said Brigham Young. "Our Father in Heaven begat all the spirits that ever were, or ever will be, upon this earth; and they were born spirits in the eternal world."[16]

One of the most able expositors of this doctrine of preexistence was Apostle Orson Pratt. In 1853, Pratt published *The Seer*, elaborating upon ideas expressed in his 1849 treatise "The Absurdities of Immaterialism" and his 1851 pamphlet "The Great First Cause." Building upon Joseph Smith's modified materialism, Pratt constructed an ultra-materialistic system reminiscent of the thought of Gottfried Leibniz in which all matter necessarily existed in the form of ultimately indivisible particles possessing a degree of inherent intelligence.[17] In the course of time, according to Pratt, these eternal particle entities would be "organized in the womb of the celestial female" thereby creating an individual spirit body. Thus, through spiritual pregnancy and birth, existence would begin on a new level.[18] In effect, each particle of intelligence would be analogous to a cell of a body which had its own existence but which formed another individual on an aggregate level. Spirit identity was created through spiritual birth, even though each intelligence or particle making up the spirit was uncreated. Pratt called the inherent intelligence in these primeval particles "The Great First Cause."

Despite Pratt's standing in the Quorum of Twelve Apostles, his views were almost immediately censured by Brigham Young. In response to Young's general criticism that some items in *The Seer* were not "Sound Doctrine," Pratt assumed that Young was referring to his concept of God's attributes.[19] In reality, the conflict between Pratt and Young was a much more fundamental dispute over absolutist and finitist theologies. Although Pratt's idea of eternal, individual particles would have been compatible with Young's materialistic pluralism, Pratt interpreted his doctrine as a monistic absolutism, endorsing the pantheistic concept of God.

In the ensuing years Young opposed Pratt's concept of God and rejected the implications of his opinions on preexistence. Ironically, both men no doubt believed their teachings originated with Joseph Smith. The crux of the conflict was Young's criticism that Pratt worshipped the attributes of Absolute Being rather than God the person. In turn Pratt rejected Young's ultra-personalistic view of God as an exalted man forever becoming greater in dominion and knowledge.[20] Pratt's notion of God was merely a logical corollary of his idea of preexistence particles. In Pratt's interpretation of God's attributes, the idea that all beings, including the Father and the Son, were the result of intelligent particles meant that the sum of their individual parts comprised the Intelligence of God or the essence of Deity which should be worshipped. Young stressed the importance of the person of God, not his attributes or particles. Both leaders were attempting to reconcile the parentage of spirits with Joseph Smith's apparently conflicting teachings regarding, first, the contingent existence of humans and, second, the eternal, uncreated existence of spirits, as well as his teaching that God was a man.

The conflict between Pratt and Young resulted in an official denunciation of Pratt's views by the First Presidency in 1860 and again in 1865. Specifically, Young's 1860 First Presidency objected to Pratt's idea of God's absolute omniscience and discounted the concept of a "Great First Cause." The 1865 denunciation challenged Pratt's view that "every part of the Holy Spirit, however minute and infinitesmal, possessed 'every intellectual or moral attribute possessed by the Father and the Son'" and that all beings were the result of self-organized, eternal particles of matter. On the matter of the origin of preexistent beings, the First Presidency stated that the church would have to be "content with the knowledge that *from all eternity there had been organized beings, in an organized form*, possessing superior and controlling power to govern . . . and that it was neither rational nor consistent with the revelations of God and with reason and philosophy, to believe that these latter Forces and Powers had existed prior to the Being who controlled and governed them" (emphasis added).[21]

Even though the First Presidency's statement appears to establish the doctrine that "organized being" necessarily exists, when analyzed in relation to Brigham Young's contemporary teachings, it merely indicates that there never was a time when organized beings did *not* exist. Young's idea was one of eternal regression of progenitors, the doctrine that all fathers had fathers *ad infinitum*. The statement did show that Pratt's ideas of particles as self-organizing and his notion that we should worship the Intelligence created by the sum of its parts were contrary to the church's position. Perhaps the point of both official statements was that because they could not "explain how the first organized Being originated," any attempt to do so was merely philosophical speculation.

The conflict between absolutist and finitist theologies continued after the deaths of Young and Pratt. Just three years after Pratt's death in 1881, future apostle Charles W. Penrose, then chief editor of the *Deseret News*, delivered a discourse that adopted Pratt's absolutist view of God despite the earlier statements of the First Presidency. Penrose claimed that God is omnipresent because of the Holy Spirit, "which animates all created beings." He also taught that this omnipresent spirit or Intelligence existed before the organization of the person of God. Penrose's doctrine of God also necessitated the "creation" of individual man. He explained: "The individual, the organized person may have had a beginning, but that spirit of which and by which they [were] organized never had a beginning. . . . The primal particles never had a beginning. They have been organized in different shapes; the organism had a beginning, but the atoms of which it is composed never had. . . . The elementary parts of matter as well as of spirit, using ordinary language, never had beginning."[22] Thus, Penrose's doctrine was merely Pratt's neo-absolutist pantheism.

The postmortem popularity of Pratt's doctrine, however, did not go unchallenged by the First Presidency. In 1892, in response to the teaching that "our spirits were not begotten by God but were created out of the elements," George Q. Cannon, first counselor in the First Presidency, referred to the trouble between Young and Pratt over the same issue and corrected the view "that it was right to worship intelligence that was in God the Eternal Father and not God (as an embodied person)." He distinguished between the Father and the Son, saying that we pray to the Father in the name of the Son, and refuted the idea that Deity was composed of particles, each of which possessed the attributes of God. However, neither Cannon nor church president Wilford Woodruff specifically disagreed with Pratt's doctrine of preexistence, although this was implied in the notion of God which they rejected.[23]

While the origin of human identity was rarely addressed in official discourse during the mid- to late nineteenth century, the issue of personal eternalism became a subject of much controversy in the early 1900s. The issue was addressed in *Outlines of Mormon Philosophy*, a little-known work by Lycurgus Wilson. Wilson rejected the neo-absolutist view "that spirits owe their origin to God" and concluded that "intelligences always were and always will be indi-

vidual entities, and, however varied in capacity, never had a beginning and can never be annihilated."[24] Wilson's work was reportedly
reviewed by an official church committee and was published by the
Deseret News Publishing Company, the publishing arm of the Mormon church.

B. H. Roberts, one of the seven presidents of the Quorum of
the Seventy, also took exception to the neo-absolutist view that man,
as an autonomous individual, was created or begotten. Elaborating
on views expressed in his *New Witness for God*, Roberts claimed that
even before spiritual birth and consequent organization of a spirit
body, man existed as an individual, autonomous and self-conscious
entity known as an intelligence. The First Presidency allowed
Roberts to publish his views in the *Improvement Era* in April 1907 with
their appended approval: "Elder Roberts submitted the following
paper to the First Presidency and a number of the Twelve Apostles,
none of whom found anything objectionable in it, or contrary to the
revealed work of God, and therefore favor its publication."[25]

Roberts met with opposition when he attempted to incorporate similar views into his 1911 *Seventy's Course in Theology*. Penrose in
particular objected to Roberts's view that "intelligences were self-
existent entities before they entered into the organization of the
spirit."[26] Both Penrose and Anthon Lund, members of the First
Presidency under Joseph F. Smith, persuaded Roberts "to eliminate
his theories in regard to intelligences as conscious self-existing beings or entities before being organized into spirit." Lund recorded
in his journal, "This doctrine has raised much discussion and the
inference on which [B. H. Roberts] builds his theory is very vague.
The Prophet's [Joseph Smith] speech delivered as a funeral sermon
over King Follett is the basis of Bro. Roberts doctrine: namely, where
he speaks of man's eternity claim. Roberts wants to prove that man is
then co-eval with God."[27]

Even though Roberts agreed to remove passages referring to
intelligences before spirit birth, the *Seventy's Course in Theology* is very
explicit about individual uncreated intelligence. Roberts derived six
attributes inherent in human primal intelligence calculated to clarify eternal existence as personal identities. Roberts asserted that
much of the confusion about the subject stemmed from inexact word
usage. Noting possible equivocations of meaning, he attempted to
reconcile the pre-Nauvoo usage of terms such as "intelligence" and

"spirit" with that of the Nauvoo era, especially in the King Follett discourse. Roberts noted, "It is observed that he [Joseph Smith] uses the words 'Intelligence' and 'spirit' interchangeably—one for the other; and yet we can discern that it is the 'intelligence of spirits,' not 'spirits' entire that is the subject of his thought. It is the 'Intelligence of Spirits' that he declares uncreated and uncreatable—eternal as God is."[28]

But the First Presidency, particularly Charles Penrose, demonstrated its opposition to the idea of necessary existence through spirit birth or creation when it removed the King Follett discourse from Roberts's new edition of Joseph Smith's *History of the Church* in 1912. Penrose doubted the authenticity and correctness of the reporting of the sermon. Apostle George Albert Smith agreed that "the report of the sermon might not be authentic and I feared that it contained some things that might be contrary to the truth."[29]

At least one church member, John A. Widtsoe, accepted Roberts's theory that intelligences existed as individual entities before they were begotten as spirits. When Widtsoe incorporated this view in *A Rational Theology*, however, President Joseph F. Smith personally stopped its publication. In December 1914, Smith wired his counselor Anthon Lund from Missouri to postpone publication until he could examine its contents. Upon examination, Lund also disagreed with Widtsoe's idea "of the origin of God, which he makes an evolution from intelligences and being superior to the other He became God." Commenting on Widtsoe's doctrine, Lund said, "I do not like to think of a time when there was no God." When Smith returned to Salt Lake City on 11 December, he went over the work with Widtsoe and Lund and "eliminated from it all that pertained to intelligences before they became begotten spirits as that would only be speculation."[30]

Accordingly, Widtsoe's published *A Rational Theology* conceded that "to speculate upon the condition of man when conscious life was just dawning is most interesting, but so little is known about that far-off day that such speculation is profitless." "All that is really clear," Widtsoe cautiously affirmed, "is that man has existed 'from the beginning,' and that, from the beginning, he has possessed distinct individuality impossible of confusion with any other individuality among the hosts of intelligent beings." Like Roberts, he delineated inherent capacities of intelligences: "In addition to his power to learn and the consciousness of his own existence, the primeval personality possessed, 'from the beginning,' the distinguishing characteristics of every intelligent, conscious, thinking being—an independent and individual will."[31]

As both Lund and Penrose intimated, the consequences of accepting the idea of man's necessary existence bothered them. In contrast to the need for an infinite being absolutely in control of the universe, both Roberts and Widtsoe insisted that individual eternalism made God necessarily conditioned, a finite being. Ironically, Roberts's and Widtsoe's doctrine of individual intelligences predating spirit existence prevailed in Mormon thought despite the reluctance of the First Presidency to endorse a specific doctrine of preexistence. For instance, shortly after Widtsoe's *A Rational Theology* was published, future apostle James E. Talmage, then president of the University of Utah, affirmed, "So far as we can peer into the past by the aid of revealed light we can see that there was always a gradation of intelligence, and consequently of ability, among spirits. . . . Individualism is an attribute of the soul, and as truly eternal as the soul itself."[32]

Before his death in 1933, B. H. Roberts sought to more solidly establish the doctrine of the necessary existence of humans. In his unpublished manuscript, "The Truth, The Way, The Life," Roberts wrote, "The conception of the existence of independent, uncreated, self-existent intelligences, who by the inherent nature of them are of various degrees of intelligence, and moral quality, differing from each other in many ways, yet alike in their eternity and their freedom . . . relieves God of the responsibility for the nature and moral status of intelligences in all stages of their development."[33]

Because of disagreement among church authorities over its contents, Roberts's manuscript was never published. The committee appointed to review his work was willing to accept Roberts's definition of an "intelligence" as "that eternal entity which was not created" but could not agree with Roberts that intelligences were morally autonomous in the sense that they could "rebel against truth and God."[34] Committee members argued to the First Presidency that Roberts's "use of 'Mind, spirit and soul,' appears confusing to us" and that contrary to Roberts's claims, "intelligence as an entity . . . cannot rebel against light and truth."[35] Roberts refused to alter a single item of his manuscript requested by the committee.

The attempts of Roberts and Widtsoe to refine Mormon theology on humanity's ultimate origin was again rebuffed in 1936 by apostle Joseph Fielding Smith, son of Joseph F. Smith. While confirming the existence of pre-spirit intelligence and spirit birth, Smith criticized those who sought to define the doctrine of the church on the nature of uncreated intelligence. Probably with Roberts and Widtsoe in mind, Smith asserted, "Some of our writers have endeavored to explain what an intelligence is, but to do so is futile, for we have never been given any insight into this matter beyond what the Lord had fragmentarily revealed. We know, however, that there is something called an intelligence which always existed. It is the real eternal part of man, which is not created or made. This intelligence combined with the spirit constitutes a spiritual entity or individual. The spirit of man, then, is a combination of the intelligence and the spirit which is an entity begotten of God."[36] Smith resisted the idea that intelligence possessed individuality or self-determination. But he unknowingly capitulated on what Lund and Penrose had earlier objected to—the contingency of the human spirit.

In spite of such cautionary statements, numerous Mormon writers at least since 1940 have assumed that the eternal existence of individuals was Mormonism's official doctrine. Such is the case with Gilbert Orme, *The Four Estates of Man* (1948); Sterling McMurrin, *The Philosophical Foundations of Mormonism* (1959) and *The Theological Foundations of Mormonism* (1965); Truman Madsen, *Eternal Man* (1966); B. F. Cummings III, *The Eternal Individual Self* (1968); and to a lesser degree R. Clayton Brough, *Our First Estate* (1977). Through the 1970s, Mormon thought appeared to be well established in metaphysical pluralism and finitistic theology despite occasional rhetoric expressing faith in the vocabulary of traditional absolutism.

Since 1960, a philosophy in contrast to traditional Mormon thought has gained some popularity in Mormon circles. Known as Mormon neo-orthodoxy, it emphasizes human contingency, the creation of humankind as conscious entities, and God's absoluteness and complete otherness.[37] The most influential proponent of Mormon neo-orthodoxy was probably Apostle Bruce R. McConkie. Greatly influenced by Joseph Fielding Smith, McConkie insisted on an absolute conception of God and also maintained that "intelligence or spirit element became intelligences *after* the spirits were born as individual entities."[38] In response to an inquiry regarding the official position of the church on the status of intelligences before spiritual birth, McConkie said, "As far as I know there is no official pronouncement on the subject at hand. . . . In my judgment there was no agency prior to spirit birth and we did not exist as entities until that time."[39]

Whenever the issue of humanity's eternal existence has been raised by writers of church priesthood or auxiliary lessons in recent years, the matter has been officially branded as speculation and deleted from lesson manuals.[40] The conflict between absolute and finite theologies has yet to be satisfactorily resolved in Mormon thought.

The idea of human necessary existence has not always characterized Mormon theology, and even when it has, the philosophical strength of the doctrine has rarely been appreciated. But the doctrine is a foundation upon which a consistent and unique theology has been built. The belief that humans necessarily exist provides philosophical justification for the idea that they may ultimately become like God. It stresses the positive aspects of human existence, rejects the dogma of original sin and salvation by grace alone, and emphasizes works and personal ability to do good. It accentuates freedom of the will, explains the existence of evil and the purpose of life, and, most importantly, asserts that God is a personal being conditioned by and related to the physical universe.

— NOTES —

1. S. N. D. Kelly, *Early Christian Doctrine* (New York: Harper and Row, 1978), 175, 345–46.

2. See, for example, Apostle Parley P. Pratt's statement that at death the human spirit "return[s] to the fountain and become[s] part of the great all from which [it] emanated," in Parker Pratt Robinson, *Writings of Parley P. Pratt* (Salt Lake City: Robinson, 1952), 216.

3. Book of Mormon and early Mormon theology tended toward binitarianism; the Son was a manifestation of the Father, not necessarily a separate being. See Boyd Kirkland, "The Development of the Mormon Doctrine of God," in this volume.

4. Bonaventura Mariani in "Genesi," *La Sacra Biblia* (Milano: Gaizanti Edition, 1964): 17–18.

5. See Bruce R. McConkie, *Mormon Doctrine* (Salt Lake City: Bookcraft, 1966), 290.

6. *Journal of Discourses*, 26 vols. (Liverpool: Latter-day Saints' Book Depot, 1855–86), 15:249; hereafter JD.

7. The transition between these verses is the juncture of the Yahwist (J) narrative and the priestly (P) account of the Creation, the so-called P-J seam, which the King James translators glossed over.

8. Origen accepted the doctrine of human preexistence and treated Genesis 1:1–2:4 as a conceptual blueprint. See Manilo Simonetti, "Alcune Osservazioni sull' interpretazione Oregeniana de Genisi," *Aevum* 36 (1972): 370–81. Philo Judaeus also accepted the notion of a spiritual creation prior to the actual creation as a conceptual blueprint. See *De opiticio mundi* 46, 34; *Legatio All.* I. xii, 31.

9. B. H. Roberts, ed., *History of the Church*, 7 vols. (Salt Lake City: Deseret Book, 1965), 5:392–93; Andrew F. Ehat and Lyndon W. Cook, *The Words of Joseph Smith* (Provo, UT: Brigham Young University Religious Studies Center, 1980), 351. Anthony Hutchinson has argued that the Book of Moses intended "real" preexistence as opposed to ontologically mind-independent or "ideal" preexistence, citing Moses 3:5: "the Lord God had created all the children of men . . . for in heaven I created them" (p. 37n15). However, this overlooks Doctrine and Covenants 29 as an aid to interpreting Moses. Further, the parallels which Hutchinson thought suggested real premortal existence do not clearly refer to anything more than a plan in the mind of God to create in his own image. Finally, D&C 93 almost certainly refers to ideal premortal existence, and it is unlikely that Smith formulated and then retreated from the notion of real premortal existence. It is more logical to assume that he was consistent during this period in teaching a spiritual creation, or divine prescience, that predated the idea of spiritual creation, and that the later concept evolved gradually.

10. Charles R. Harrell, "The Development of the Doctrine of Preexistence, 1830–1844," *Brigham Young University Studies* 28 (Spring 1988): 77, 43n20.

11. See Hutchinson, 65.

12. Robinson, 66–67; Harrell, 84.

13. See, for example, *Messenger and Advocate* 1 (April 1835): 97.

14. Compare Anthony A. Hutchinson, "A Mormon Midrash? LDS Creation Narratives Reconsidered," *Dialogue: A Journal of Mormon Thought* 21 (Winter 1988): 51.

15. See Ehat and Cook, 207, 60. Smith's January 1841 statement demonstrates that the "organization of spirits" in the Book of Abraham refers to an organization into a heavenly council and not to an organization of an intelligence through spiritual birth resulting in an "organized spirit":

"Spirits are eternal. At the first organization in heaven we were all present and saw the Savior chosen and appointed, and the plan of salvation made and we sanctioned it" (ibid., 60). Smith similarly stated in May 1843: "The design of God before the foundation of the world was that we should take tabernacles . . . inasmuch as the Spirits of the Eternal World, glory in bringing other Spirits in Subjection unto them, striving continually for the mastery, He who rules the heavens when he has a certain work to do calls the Spirits before him to organize them. They present themselves and offer their services" (ibid., 207). This same point is made by Harrell.

16. Fred C. Collier, ed., *The Teachings of President Brigham Young* (Salt Lake City: Collier's Publishing Co., 1987), 3:92.

17. See T. Edgar Lyon, "Orson Pratt: Early Mormon Leader," M.A. thesis, University of Chicago, 1932, 102–19; cf. Gottfried Leibniz, "The Monadology," in *The Rationalists* (New York: Anchor Books, 1974), trans. Albert Chandler, 455–71.

18. See Orson Pratt, *The Seer* (Washington, D.C., 1853), 102–103.

19. Brigham Young to Orson Pratt, 1 Sept. 1853, archives, Historical Department, Church of Jesus Christ of Latter-day Saints, Salt Lake City, Utah, hereafter church archives; Orson Pratt to Brigham Young, 4 Nov. 1853, church archives.

20. See Gary James Bergera, "The Orson Pratt-Brigham Young Controversies: Conflict Within the Quorums, 1853 to 1868," *Dialogue: A Journal of Mormon Thought* 13 (Summer 1980), 2:7–49.

21. Both official statements are in James R. Clark, ed., *Messages of the First Presidency of the Church of Jesus Christ of Latter-day Saints*, 6 vols. (Salt Lake City: Bookcraft, 1965–75), 2:214–24, 229–40; the quotes are from pp. 232–33.

22. Charles Penrose, in JD 26:17.

23. See St. George, Utah, Stake High Council Minutes, 11 June 1892, church archives.

24. Lycurgus A. Wilson, *Outline of Mormon Philosophy* (Salt Lake City: Deseret News Publishing Company, 1905), 42.

25. B. H. Roberts, "The Immortality of Man," *Improvement Era*, April 1907, 401–23.

26. Anthon H. Lund Journal, 25 Aug. 1911, church archives.

27. Ibid., 29 Aug. 1911.

28. B. H. Roberts, *The Seventy's Course in Theology* (Salt Lake City: Deseret News Publishing Company, 1911), 11.

29. See Donald Q. Cannon, "The King Follett Discourse: Joseph Smith's Greatest Sermon in Historical Perspective," *Brigham Young University Studies* 18 (1978): 191n61, n62.

30. Lund Journal, 7, 11 Dec. 1914.

31. John A. Widtsoe, *A Rational Theology* (Salt Lake City: Deseret Book, 1915), 24–25, 16, 17.

32. James E. Talmage, *The Vitality of Mormonism* (Boston: Gorham Press, 1919), 321.

33. B. H. Roberts, "The Truth, The Way, The Life," chap. 26, Special Collections, Marriott Library, University of Utah, Salt Lake City.

34. George Albert Smith to Rudger Clawson, 10 Oct. 1929, church archives.

35. In Rudger Clawson to Heber J. Grant, 15 May 1930, church archives.

36. Joseph Fielding Smith, *The Progress of Man* (Salt Lake City: Utah Genealogical Society, 1936), 11.

37. See O. Kendall White, Jr., *Mormon Neo-Orthodoxy: A Crisis Theology* (Salt Lake City: Signature Books, 1987).

38. McConkie, 387.

39. Bruce R. McConkie to Walter Horme, 2 Oct. 1974, copy in my possession.

40. Ibid.

13.
The Traditional Mormon Doctrine of Man

George Boyd

THAT MAN — MEANING ALL HUMANITY — IS ESSENTIALLY GOOD BY nature is one of the primary proclamations of the Church of Jesus Christ of Latter-day Saints. This positive assessment, which underlies and determines the contemporary Mormon doctrine of salvation, is implicit in the church's teachings relative to our original uncreated status in the universe, our present moral and spiritual possibilities in this world, and the exaltation we may achieve in the hereafter. The optimistic tone of the Mormon doctrine of man becomes clear when contrasted with the pessimism inherent in the doctrines of the Fall, original sin, and total human depravity of traditional Christian theology.

Because I use the term "optimism" to describe the Mormon concept of man, it may be helpful to distinguish between two related meanings of the term before attempting to answer the central question: How is innate human nature to be defined or described within the context of Mormon theology? First, "optimism" may be employed in a general way to characterize Mormonism's acceptance of this world as a God-given blessing and opportunity. This attitude finds confirmation in Mormon scripture. After discussing Adam's role in initiating God's plan in this world, Nephi, a Book of Mormon prophet, states, "But behold, all things have been done in the wisdom of him who knoweth all things. Adam fell that men might be; and men are, that they might have joy" (2 Ne. 2:24, 25). From this passage it is evident that the Fall was neither an accident nor an infringement of God's plan. Nor did it result in the moral corruption of human nature. "Corruption" in Mormon discourse refers to the physical degeneration of the biological organism and certainly not to the Christian doctrine of inherited sin and guilt. This does not mean that man is not morally corruptible but that moral corruptibility is not a result of the Fall. In the immediate context from which the above passage is taken, Nephi rejoices in the fall of man and the blessings of mortality. Mortality constitutes the second estate, a God-given opportunity for further growth and fulfillment.

In stressing this point it is not to be understood that the Mormon attitude toward the world is superficial or blind to real evil in the world. Mormon optimism is not escapism but the faith that in spite of the dark side of life the world and humans belong together, that both are capable of perfection, and that within the framework of God's plan the perfection of each depends upon an interplay in which the moral, intellectual, and spiritual efforts of humanity make a real difference to the final outcome. Mormonism affirms the world, even though it may not be "the best of all possible worlds," and accepts the challenge and task of trying to improve it and to enlarge the human soul. The role of God in relation to man and the world is a presupposed necessary condition to the realization of these possibilities.

This affirmative attitude toward the world is part of what is meant by Mormon optimism. But the term as employed here stands for a doctrine of human nature that holds man to be essentially good by nature. The term "pessimism" stands for the opposing view that man is evil by nature. ("Neutralism" is the position that man is neither good nor bad by nature but neutral and that how he turns out is determined by the conditions under which he lives. While it may be possible to make a case for neutralism within the context of Mormon theology, it is not dealt with here as it fails to express important aspects of Mormon theology.)

Any definition or description of human nature within the framework of Mormon theology must be guided by a number of basic ideas, including: the notion of a nonabsolutistic God, which includes the idea that God has achieved divinity by progressing through time; the doctrine that man is of the same species as God and in his ultimate nature is uncreated, self-existent, and coeternal with God; the belief that reality, including our physical world, is dynamic and capable of progressing; and the position that there is no sharp bifurcation of reality into the natural and the supernatural, with the result that the natural order described by time and space is continuous and includes both God and humans.

If truth is defined in terms of knowledge, then the truth about the nature of man must include what is known of his past (or premortal existence), his present (or mortal existence), and his future (or postmortal existence). Therefore, any description of the Mormon view of man based solely on what is known of him in mortality will be fragmented. For example, the moral nature of man cannot be described solely in terms of "the Fall." In fact, "the Fall" must be understood in terms of the eternal existence of man. Man is a "becoming" as well as a "being." His destiny as well as his origin, his potentiality as well as actuality, must figure in any description of his total nature within the context of Mormonism.

The knowledge we possess of man in the preexistence is limited and based principally upon what is found in Mormon scripture. Yet these scriptures tell us considerable and imply a great deal more. Among other things all human beings are said to have been in the beginning with God as uncreated, self-existing egos, or "intelligences." The ground of their being, therefore, is in themselves, giving them permanent ontological status in the universe.

These primordial selves, or "intelligences," must be defined in terms of the same psychic activities or functions, such as thinking, willing, feeling, which define the individual, however embryonic these functions may have been; otherwise there seems to be no basis for the continuity of the individual through eternity, which in Mormonism means endless time. It was the presence of these functions, either actually or potentially, that made it possible for God to enlarge the experience of "intelligences" by bringing them into a "spiritual estate." The original "intelligences," or centers of consciousness, were then clothed with spiritual bodies which made possible a greater range of activity. Living as a community of spirits, opportunities for mental, moral, and emotional developments were increased. Spirits were free agents, capable of making moral commitments and capable of breaking them. As free agents they had the power to distinguish good from bad and were responsible for their choices.

There came a time in this "spiritual estate" when opportunities for further development were exhausted. The Father revealed
his plan for a mortal experience to his children. This was rejected by
Lucifer and a vast number of other spirits, all of whom were cast out
of God's presence and deprived of the opportunities of mortality.
Those who accepted God's plan rejoiced in anticipation of their
mortal existence as an opportunity for further development.

Now, what can be said of the moral nature of man in his
pre-earth life? Let it be remembered that the possession of rational
and volitional power implies that he had a moral nature. Was that
nature essentially good or evil, and on what grounds is one to say
that by nature pre-earth spirits were inclined toward good or evil?
On the basis of conduct reported in Mormon scripture some spirits
were good and some evil (Abr. 3:22–28; D&C 29:36). Is the reported
fact of evil conduct grounds for a doctrine of "pessimism"? Is the
reported fact of good conduct grounds for a doctrine of "optimism"?

It is difficult to imagine any Latter-day Saint holding that all
spirits were evil by nature. This characterization, when used, is reserved for mortal man. Yet, if evil is thought of in terms of that which
is contrary to the will of God, certainly all pre-earth individuals, as
well as all mortals, were capable of evil. And, just as mortal man is
actually involved in evil, vast numbers of the spirits in the preexistence were involved in evil. The fact that Lucifer and his followers, as
spirits, were evil should invalidate the widely held notion that devil-
ishness in humanity is necessarily a derivative of carnality and sensuousness. Neither carnality nor sensuousness nor sensuality, for
that matter, can be ascribed to Satan for he possesses neither a
physical body nor physical senses as man does, yet he is devilish.
This means that the traditional moral dualism which sets the spirit
as being good against the flesh as being evil is a misconception and
is inadequate to explain either the good or bad in humans. What is
important here is that the unembodied spirit itself, as a free agent,
was capable of doing evil in the preexistence and therefore evil in
humans is not necessarily a derivative of the Fall or of our carnal and
sensuous nature.

It is obvious that the original "intelligences" always possessed the potential of becoming spirits, for such they became. It also
follows (from the doctrine of the uncreated nature of "intelligences"
coupled with the doctrine of individual continuity and identity

throughout all time) that, however dependent upon God, all future development was potentially present in the original "intelligence." As a spiritual "child of God," pre-earth man inherited further attributes and possibilities of becoming like his heavenly father. And mortality was anticipated as a necessary means for moving onward toward that ultimate goal.

From the Mormon point of view, all we know about pre-earth life suggests that a dynamic expansiveness characterized life in the preexistence just as it characterizes life in mortality. This dynamic expansiveness or drive toward integrated wholeness, which simply means in Mormon terms the inherent power within man to become like God, is the key to understanding the true nature of humanity in its preexistence and, for that matter, in its present and future existence as well. It follows, therefore, that since the highest potential in pre-earth man was to become godlike, this potential revealed pre-earth humanity's true nature even though it was impossible for them to reach their full stature in the spiritual state. In answer, then, to the question raised above relative to the moral nature of preexistent man, it must be said that he was good by nature, because, as we have seen, it was his nature to become godlike. To say that he was bad by nature would be equivalent to saying that to have the power to become like God is bad.

If the question is how is one to account for the evil of Lucifer and his followers on the basis of a doctrine of innate goodness, the answer is that the fact of actual evil exhibited by the rebellious spirits does not prejudice the question relative to the capacities for good with which they were naturally endowed. It does not necessarily follow that because evil was present in pre-earth man that evil was the true expression of his nature. From the Mormon point of view, only good was expressive of man's total nature in the spirit world. Evil then, as now, was evidence of fragmentation, abnormality, and stunted growth and was thus unnatural because it thwarted the natural fulfillment of the spirit children of God.

With some exceptions, it has been common practice among Christians to refer to man in this life as the "natural man." In this usage the word "natural" is employed not only as the opposite in meaning to the word "spiritual" but also to indicate a basic metaphysical and moral opposition of the natural to the spiritual. Generally in Christian thought the word "natural" describes the material world, including humans as biological organisms, and connotes evil. The word "spiritual" describes the supernatural realm to which the spirit belongs but from which it is temporarily exiled and as such "spiritual" connotes the good.

In the following attempt to describe the natural or mortal man from the Mormon point of view, it will be seen that Mormonism insists that moral and spiritual laws, represented in the command-ments of God, are not merely prescriptive but also descriptive of the conditions of personal and social development in this life and as such are as inexorable and as natural as the laws of the physical world. While we must abandon traditional meanings in our efforts to define the human condition within the context of Mormonism, there seems to be no reason why we cannot make use of the term "natural man." In fact, we have already employed the word "natural" in refer-ence to man in our discussion of his preexistent state. And the appropriateness or perhaps even the necessity of using these terms in any treatment of the Mormon view of the preexistence argues against the natural/supernatural dichotomy of orthodox Christian thought and suggests something of the character of the non-dualistic position of Mormonism. I shall therefore use the term "natural man" but attempt to give it a distinctive Mormon meaning.

Perhaps the most quoted passage of Mormon scripture and the most misused in this connection is the statement of King Benjamin, "For the natural man is an enemy to God" (Mos. 3:9). The first question to be settled is what Benjamin meant by the term "natural man." It may also be asked whether Benjamin's appraisal of man is to be taken as final without weighing it against what other religious leaders have had to say on the subject. Another question is whether we are limited to the meaning Benjamin chose to give to the expression "natural man."

This passage is generally misunderstood because of the er-roneous assumption that the phrase "the natural man" includes all mortals as enemies to God simply because of their humanity, but we will see that Benjamin taught that some men are enemies to God and that others are not. Therefore, the term "natural man" as used by him does not mean a universal class into which all fall as enemies to God because they are human, but the term applies to a limited class who are enemies to God because they have chosen to disobey the Divine Will. In other words, Benjamin's meaning of "natural man" can be understood only in terms of what he meant by "an enemy to God."

A careful reading of this statement, coupled with Mosiah 2:36–38 which follows, supports the position just stated and clarifies Benjamin's meaning: "And now, I say unto you, my brethren, that after ye have known and have been taught all these things, if ye should transgress and go contrary to that which has been spoken, . . . I say unto you, that the man that doeth this, the same cometh out in open rebellion against God; therefore he listeth to obey the evil spirit, and becometh an enemy to all righteousness . . . " It is significant that King Benjamin says, "After ye have known and have been taught these things . . . " The meaning seems clear. The term "natural man" as employed by Benjamin is equivalent to "incorrigible sinner." It is also clear that all men are not included in this category. Furthermore, it is clear that those who are outside the class to which the "natural man" belongs include not only those who have not heard the gospel but also all those who have not become enemies to God by the process he described. Sin, here, has to do with acts, not with an inherent condition of depravity due to the Fall. To interpret these passages otherwise is to ascribe to Mormonism a doctrine of original sin.

This meaning finds support in Alma's statement, "all men that are in a state of nature, or I would say, in a carnal state, are in the gall of bitterness and in the bonds of iniquity" (Al. 41:11). The important point here is that the phrase "all men that are in a state of nature" seems to imply that some men are not in a state of nature, which state is the condition of those who "have gone contrary to the nature of God" and not an original condition of all born into mortality.

Statements of Benjamin suggesting that man is nothing and worthless (see Mos. 4:4) are assumed to be incompatible with the Mormon position. It might be argued that man is worthless without the help of God because he is helplessly and eternally lost. The Mormon answer is that it is because of the intrinsic worth of humanity that God is so ready and anxious to save us. The infant in the crib might also be said to be worthless in that it has done nothing for its parents or that it is absolutely helpless and would be nothing without their attention. But the child is of infinite value and as a person not only evokes the highest human responses from its parents but also fulfills their deepest needs. (It is strange that some men and women degrade themselves before the Creator, feeling, paradoxically, that they honor God by emphasizing the baseness of the creature he has made in his own image.)

The word "natural," as it is frequently used in ethical discourse, is highly ambiguous and has come to mean almost nothing because it has come to mean almost everything. The word "natural" often stands for whatever transpires or happens to be. It is said, for example, that it is natural for man to kill but that it is also natural for man to discipline himself so that he refrains from killing. Since these forms of behavior are equally natural in that they frequently occur in human experience, the word "natural" in this sense has little meaning, and distinctions between good and bad are obliterated. In this sense it was natural for the Nazis to torture their victims or for the reprobate to seduce his neighbor's wife. We mention this not only to clarify the meaning of "natural" but also to warn against identifying the Mormon position because of its naturalistic characteristics with hedonistic philosophies.

The Mormon position is that the whole man, body and spirit, constitutes man in mortality. The nature of anything, including mortal man, is determined by its essential character or constitution. Therefore, the spiritual factor cannot be ignored in any adequate description of man's essential nature. We will therefore use the term "natural man" to mean man as he is constituted of body and spirit in mortality.

An important aspect of determining whether the good or the bad expresses the moral nature of man is the relation of function to responsibility. A plant, for example, has certain functioning powers in relation to its environment. If it fails to use its functioning powers it exhibits an abnormal and therefore unnatural condition. A plant, of course, is not conscious nor free to function or not to function in accordance with its environment. Man, however, is free and can determine how he will respond to his environment, and the presence of spiritual and rational powers within him demands that he function spiritually and rationally if he is to live a normal and moral life. Not overlooking emotional and biological needs, only spiritual and rational functioning together can insure the achievement of man's ultimate destiny. For to achieve his ultimate destiny is to act in accordance with his total nature.

The natural man then is the righteous man. And to live naturally means to live in accordance with moral and spiritual laws, the observance of which actualizes divine potential. The sinful life is the unnatural life because sinfulness thwarts the growth and fulfill-ment of man. We believe, therefore, that he who conforms his life to the will of God is involved in a natural process and is giving the highest and truest expression of his nature. Thus Brigham Young commented, "Paul says in his Epistle to the Corinthians, 'But the natural man receiveth not the things of God,' but I say it is the unnatural 'man that receiveth not the things of God.' ... The natural man is of God. We are the natural sons and daughters of our natural parents, and spiritually we are the natural children of The Father of light and natural heirs to his kingdom ... Man, the noblest work of God, was in his creation designed for endless duration, for which the love of all good was incorporated in his nature. It was never designed that he should naturally do and love evil" (*Journal of Discourses*, 26 vols. [Liverpool: S. W. Richards, 1855–86], 9:305).

If the question arises as to why the natural man so often falls short of the full capacity of his spiritual and rational powers, it must be said that freedom is the only condition under which personal fulfillment is won. It is only by the voluntary operation of the will in choosing the right over the wrong, the good over the evil, that man moves toward his ultimate goal. If man has the potential to become godlike, it must be through the free, normal functioning of all his powers. With such freedom man may sink to lower levels of action, thus perverting his nature. Divine attributes and capacities demand the divine life, and these highest attributes of human nature deter-mine man's fullest, truest nature. As a free agent, man is responsible for his choices and becomes whatever he chooses to be. That some, perhaps a majority, will never achieve full stature in this life is not a valid argument for "pessimism" nor does it invalidate the claim that it is within the natural man's capacity to move in the direction of the ultimate ideal, God.

It may seem that the foregoing indicates that man's potential is contingent. But contingency—or dependence—does not mean impotence or depravity. The fact that man recognizes the need for God's help and may assume an attitude of receptivity toward him should not lead to self-depreciation and false humility. A genuine, reverent attitude toward God and insight into his relationship to humanity does not find expression in scoffing man's capacity but in the kind of moral and spiritual behavior, growing out of both a sense of personal worth and a sense of self-subordination, which bespeaks the dignity of man as a child of God.

The Mormon doctrine of the Atonement holds that humanity is totally dependent on God for future fulfillment. But Mormonism also holds that although the Atonement is a necessary condition for salvation, it is not a sufficient condition for the fulfillment we refer to as exaltation. At least part of the meaning of the worth and dignity of humanity must reside in the fact that man, as a moral agent, is responsible for his own growth and development. Certainly little worth or dignity could be ascribed to a person, however exalted his status, if that position was not in some way the product of his own efforts. In Mormon doctrine Satan seems to have erred on this point, for he thought that he could save humanity in the absence of human freedom and effort.

The Mormon doctrine of the Atonement and humanity's dependence on God are not grounds for pessimism but, as indicated, constitute a strong argument for optimism. Pessimism as an ethical theory is frequently based upon the evil behavior detected in humans. But the debatable question is the identification of the observed fact of evil with a doctrine of human nature.

For Mormonism, human freedom includes the power to will the good. We must give expression to all our functioning powers, including our rational and spiritual powers, if we are to live naturally. To live solely on the physical or biological level may be natural for animals, but it is unnatural for humans. The natural man is not dominated by sensuous pleasures. The natural man's life is both rational and spiritual. If Jesus Christ is to be taken as the inspiration and norm, then the fruits of his spirit—love, joy, peace, and long-suffering—are the normal products of the fully functioning soul and written into nature as a part of the constitution of reality. The possession of capacities for spiritual living is the proof of man's nascent divinity.

Mormonism rejects the doctrine that the physical body, as such, is evil. From the Mormon position the Fall did not change the moral nature of man essentially but was an act calculated to actualize potentialities eternally present in him. That the possession of a physical body may make possible additional ways of sinning in no way alters the basic moral structure of man. It is simply one of the conditions on which the ultimate fulfillment of man rests. The perpetuation of the union of the body and the spirit is so important for the fulfillment and perfection of man in Mormon thought that the one automatic and inevitable result of the Atonement is the resurrection, assuring the reunion of the body with the spirit after their separation by death.

While Mormonism is aware of the vast amount of moral evil in the world and is conscious of its own responsibility to help diminish and overcome evil, it does not hold that moral improvement is achieved by radically changing human nature. To improve morally cannot mean to change what we call human nature into something else or to cease being involved in those impulses and drives, frequently described as evil, without which we would not only cease to be human but cease to exist altogether. Moral improvement in Mormonism is to be achieved by bringing all the facets of human nature into proper balance with each other and the whole person into proper relationship with his total environment, which includes God. To improve morally means to bring drives and habits under the dominion of the rational and spiritual powers of human nature so that the significance of good and evil, right and wrong, in relation to the expanding personality is understood.

Nature is not an enemy to God. The various drives — hunger, thirst, sex, combativeness, acquisitiveness, and others — which supply biological needs are all essential to life and as such are good. All of these drives are capable of a high degree of functional malleability in human living. Hunger may turn to gluttony, thirst to drunkenness, acquisitiveness to theft, and sex to lust. Nevertheless, each of these drives is also capable of modifications in the other direction. For example, sex at the physiological level may be nothing more than a biological function. But at a higher level, as an act of genuine love, it is capable of reaching lofty psychological and spiritual dimensions of expression.

What is so frequently overlooked in ascribing evil to the physical nature of humans is the fact that nature both internal and external to man is ever ready to collaborate with him in his task of self-fulfillment. Nature's hand is not set against God but responds to the will of God as it relates to humanity's progress and growth. The natural life, as it has been described to include the physical and

spiritual in proper balance, is the abundant life of which Jesus
Christ spoke, because it brings self-fulfillment. And progressive self-
fulfillment is the only source of lasting joy. The Book of Mormon
teaches that "men are that they might have joy," and in the achievement of joy the physical body is an essential element.

In any discussion of the future life from the Mormon point
of view, a clarification of the Mormon concept of time is necessary.
Contrary to the notion commonly held in theological circles that
time is a product of God's creation sandwiched between the timeless
eternities of past and future, Mormonism holds that eternity is endless time including the past, present, and future. Consistent with this
is the belief that movement, progression, and retrogression are also
real. God is in time and is time-conscious, having himself progressed
through time. Thus Mormons look forward to a life after death
where growth and progress are possible. Heaven is not a place of
inactivity but one of enlarged opportunities for the soul's further
fulfillment.

Mormon optimism relative to the future life is seen in the
rejection of any notion of predestination and in the doctrine of
universal resurrection and salvation. The Mormon view is that with
few exceptions men and women born into this life will not only be
saved but will share a future of varying degrees of glory, the three
main divisions of which are known as celestial, terrestrial, and
telestial, where almost all men and women will have the chance to
move forward eternally in their drive for fulfillment.

Mormonism does not hold that sinners will not suffer the
effects of their sins. Both rewards and punishments are natural consequences, and the repentant, forgiven sinner in the hereafter may
find himself greatly retarded. Yet however handicapped by the effects of previous sin, there is always the opportunity to move forward. With endless time before him there would seem to be no limit
to the end a person can achieve.

Mormon scripture as it portrays the future of man testifies to
the achievement of this high status, at least by those who inherit the
celestial kingdom: "These are they into whose hands the Father has
given all things—they are they who are priests and kings, who have
received of his fulness, and of his glory; . . . Wherefore, as it is written, they are gods, even the sons of God" (D&C 76:55–58). Thus

humans, according to Mormon scripture, are by nature good and may eventually achieve godhood.

The foregoing survey of humanity's past, present, and future within the context of Mormon thought leads, I believe, to the conclusion that optimism characterizes the traditional Mormon concept of man and that this is the only description consistent with fundamental Mormon doctrines.

14.
Salvation in the Theology of Joseph Smith

David John Buerger

PRIOR TO MID-1831, MORMON TEACHINGS ON SALVATION DO NOT seem to have been Calvinistic despite Book of Mormon teachings regarding the "natural man" and God's chosen people. References to God's elect, a limited atonement, salvation for the "predestined," and the doctrine of "calling and election" are conspicuously absent and even argued against (see Al. 31:16–17). The Doctrine and Covenants's sole use of the phrase "calling and election" appeared in a June 1831 revelation (D&C 53:1, 7) which was similarly free from eschatological implications.

At some point between June and November 1831, however, LDS teachings regarding the concept of salvation changed. A precipitating event seems to been the 3 June 1831 conferral of the "High Priesthood" on church elders.[1] According to testimony in 1887 by Book of Mormon witness David Whitmer, the introduction of high priests, an event he considered to be an unfortunate aberration from scriptural sources, "originated in the mind of Sidney Rigdon," Joseph Smith's close associate: "Rigdon finally persuaded Brother Joseph to believe that the high priests which had such great power in ancient times, should be in the Church of Christ to-day. He had Brother Joseph inquire of the Lord about it, and they received an answer according to their erring desires."[2] Official church histories contain no record of the kind of disagreement or controversy Whitmer here alludes to, and the significance of the event may have been perceived differently as time passed.

The new office of high priest quickly came to be regarded as different from and greater than those of priest and elder, both of which already existed in the new church, because a high priest could "seal," that is, perform earthly ordinances which were unconditionally ratified in heaven. Joseph Smith spelled out this crucial function on 25 October 1831, when he reportedly said at a conference in Far West, Missouri: "The order of the High-priesthood is that they have power given them to seal up the Saints unto eternal life. And said it was the privilege of every Elder present to be ordained to the High priesthood."[3]

The far-reaching implications of this teaching went beyond biblical precedents which seemed to use the same terminology in a related sense. In the New Testament, for example, the terms "to seal" and "to place a seal on" metaphorically reflected the ancient practice of placing a wax or clay seal on a document to close and protect it from misappropriation. The confirming effect of a "sealing" is seen in several Pauline passages where God "seals" Christians by giving them the Holy Spirit or the Holy Spirit of Promise as a ratification of future blessings and promises to come (see Rom. 4:11; 2 Cor. 1:22; Eph. 1:13, 4:30). The Revelation of John graphically depicts the servants of God receiving the seal or imprint of God in their foreheads (Rev. 13:16–18). In all pertinent New Testament references, however, it is God alone who applies the seal; there is no clear reference to a human intermediary as part of the "sealing" function.

The sixteenth-century Reformation used many of these "sealing" passages to support a belief in predestination. Liberal reaction to this Calvinist doctrine arose early in the seventeenth century when Arminians rejected this view, asserting instead that God's sovereignty and humanity's free will were compatible and that such "sealing" depended upon choices of individual believers. Arminian doctrines of free will and individual works continued to be propagated on the American frontier through such nineteenth-century groups as Alexander Campbell's Disciples of Christ and other primitivistic seekers. In 1829, when Joseph Smith was working on the Book of Mormon manuscript, these same issues were being discussed throughout the "Burned-over District" of western New York state.

Aside from the obvious nonmetaphorical uses of the term

"sealing"—for example, "sealing up" a book or plates, or hiding an object—the Book of Mormon generally employed the term much like the New Testament. Mosiah 5:15, for example, closely follows New Testament usage but extends the meaning by clearly emphasizing works: "I would that you should be steadfast and immovable, always abounding in good works, that Christ the Lord God Omnipotent, may seal you his, that you may be brought to Heaven." Alma 34:35 counters predestinarian ideas by warning: "If ye have procrastinated the day of your repentance, even until death, behold, ye have become subjected to the spirit of the Devil, and he doth seal you his; . . . and this is the final state of the wicked."

The most significant development in Book of Mormon sealing theology was God's power granted to Nephi, the son of Helaman: "Whatsoever ye shall seal on earth shall be sealed in heaven; and whatsoever ye shall loose on earth, shall be loosed in heaven" (He. 10:7).[4] This passage parallels Jesus' injunction to Peter in Matthew 16:17-19: "Blessed art thou, Simon Barjona . . . Whatsoever thou shalt bind on earth shall be bound in heaven; and whatsoever thou shalt loose on earth shall be loosed in heaven." The shift from the biblical *bind* to the Book of Mormon *seal*—probably to remove "papist" associations in the text—was accompanied by soteriological and eschatological changes. Nephi performs miraculous physical events, through this sealing power, such as commanding a drought which will cause a famine (He. 11:4) to bring people to repentance. Thus, the Book of Mormon modifies the concept of sealing to allow a *human* agent (Nephi) to seal literally, as well as a demonic agent (the Devil) to seal metaphorically, whereas the New Testament has only God sealing and then strictly in a symbolic sense of the term. Associating a human with this power allowed Joseph Smith to introduce a whole set of theological innovations.

In this context, the 1831 ordination of high priests was significant. In November 1831 these two concepts merged in a priesthood ritual that allowed ordained high priests to "seal [persons] up unto eternal life" (D&C 68:2, 12; 1:8-9) or to eternal or unconditional salvation. Thus, Mormon priesthood bearers themselves could perform a ritual paralleling what strict Calvinists, for example, reserved solely to God. Zebedee Coltrin's 1831 missionary diary provides evidence that Mormon elders wasted no time in implementing this ordinance: "Tuesday came to Shalersville held a meeting in the

Evening with the Br[ethren] and after laboring with them some length of time Br David seeled them up unto Eternal life."[5] An empowered priesthood bearer could thus seal not only an individual but a whole group of people to guaranteed salvation. This seems to have been spoken ritual; no physical contact between the officiator and the recipients is mentioned.[6]

A second development in Mormon salvation theology came in an 1832 revelation (D&C 88) commanding that a "School of the Prophets" be established to instruct church leaders. After describing a format for greeting members of the school, the revelation added that no one was to be admitted unless he was "clean from the blood of this generation": "And he shall be received by the ordinance of the washing of feet, for unto this end was the ordinance of washing of feet instituted." The School of the Prophets was established in late January 1833, and this ordinance was administered as directed.[7] The revelation did not explicitly state any relationship between the ordinance of washing feet and the ritual of "sealing" which had been practiced for over a year, but Smith indicated that in addition to being "clean from the blood of this generation," participants in the washing of feet were "sealed up unto eternal life."[8]

The concepts of "sealing up unto eternal life" and cleansing one's self "from the blood of this generation" reached momentary fruition in the Kirtland, Ohio, temple rituals. Doctrine and Covenants 88:119 had commanded the Saints to establish a "house of God," and six months later, on 1 June, God rebuked Joseph Smith for failing to begin construction of a house where God would "endow those whom I have chosen with power from on high" (D&C 95:8). While work on the Kirtland temple thereafter proceeded apace, even before the dedication on 27 March 1836 Smith introduced the promised new ordinances which prefaced what later was termed the Kirtland endowment. On 21 January, according to Joseph Smith's account in the *History of the Church*, the First Presidency washed their bodies in pure water and "perfumed our bodies and our heads, in the name of the Lord." They also blessed and consecrated "holy oil," which they used to seal "many blessings" on the head of Joseph Smith, Sr.[9] After several days of anointings administered to other priesthood bearers, Joseph Smith, on 6 February, "called the anointed together to receive the seal of all their blessings."[10]

A few weeks later at the dedication of the Kirtland temple,

Smith instructed various quorums regarding the ordinance of washing of feet.[11] Two days later, on 29 March, the First Presidency "proceeded to cleanse our faces and our feet, and then proceeded to wash one another's feet." After this, those in attendance "partook of the bread and wine."[12] The next day, a group of about three hundred male church members met in the temple and, after the administration of the sacrament, received the ordinance of washing of feet as well. Smith then announced that he "had now completed the organization of the Church, and we had passed through all the necessary ceremonies."[13] Just four days later, however, again in the Kirtland temple, Smith received a vision recorded in Doctrine and Covenants 110 of the prophet Elijah who gave him the full sealing power of the Melchizedek priesthood—an authority which he did not fully reveal and use until seven years later in Nauvoo, Illinois.

In early Nauvoo, Smith further expanded Mormon salvation concepts. He defined the principle of sealing people's salvation in heaven and on earth as a fulfillment of the Pauline "making your calling and election sure." In a June 1839 sermon Smith spoke of church members, following a lifetime of service and devotion, being "sealed up unto the day of redemption" while still alive, a concept based on 2 Peter 1:10–11: "Wherefore . . . brethren, give diligence to make your calling and election sure: for if ye do these things, ye shall never fall: For so an entrance shall be ministered unto you abundantly into the everlasting kingdom of our Lord and Saviour Jesus Christ" (see also 2 Pet. 1:19; Eph. 1:13–14). This June 1839 sermon[14] has additional importance, because in it Smith not only linked making one's calling and election sure to sealing theology but also added the notion of receiving a "comforter" (John 14:26), which he defined as a personal manifestation of Jesus Christ. These ideas were in turn associated with the concept of personal revelation. Smith urged the Quorum of Twelve Apostles and all Mormons to follow in his own footsteps and "become perfect in Jesus Christ." There was no reference in this sermon to a special ordinance, now associated with temple ritual; indeed there was no functioning temple at this time.

In January 1841, Smith announced another revelation. In it God asked, "How shall your washings be acceptable unto me, except ye perform them in a house which you have built to my name?" Nauvoo did not yet have a suitable structure for such activites. In addition, this new temple was needed "that I may reveal mine [higher] ordinances therein unto my people; For I deign to reveal unto my church things which have been kept hid from before the foundation of the world, things that pertain to the dispensation of the fulness of times" (D&C 124:37, 40–41). Anointed Saints were thus advised that their Kirtland ordinances were initiatory to other salvific ordinances to be revealed after a new temple was completed in Nauvoo. As before, however, these ordinances were revealed in advance by Smith to a select group of church leaders and their wives—the "Quorum of the Anointed" or "Holy Order."[15] This action proved providential, as Smith was killed nearly two years before the temple's formal dedication.

On 4 May 1842 Smith, after two days of preparation in the upper story of his store in Nauvoo, gathered together nine men: James Adams, Heber C. Kimball, William Law, William Marks, George Miller, Willard Richards, Hyrum Smith, Newel K. Whitney, and Brigham Young. There, according to the *History of the Church*, he "instruct[ed] them in the principles and order of the Priesthood, attending to washings, anointings, endowments and the communication of keys pertaining to the Aaronic Priesthood, and so on to the highest order of the Melchisedek Priesthood, setting forth the order pertaining to the Ancient of Days, and all those plans and principles by which any one is enabled to secure the fullness of those blessings which have been prepared for the Church of the First Born, and come up and abide in the presence of the Eloheim in the eternal worlds."[16]

There are some problems with this account. It is historically interesting that the *History* omits William Law and William Marks, who were present but who would later become disaffected. More significant is the statement that the "highest order of the Melchisedek Priesthood" was conferred upon these men. About four months later, in late August 1842, Smith declared to members of Nauvoo's Female Relief Society that "the Lord Almighty . . . will continue to preserve me . . . *until* I have fully accomplished my mission in life, and so firmly established the dispensation of the fullness of the priesthood in the last days, that all the power of earth and hell can never prevail against it" (emphasis added).[17] The establishment of "the fulness of the priesthood"—the crowning ordinance of developing Mormon salvation/exaltation theology—was an event Smith seems to have viewed as his future life mission, not as an accomplished fact.

Almost a year later on 6 August 1843, Apostle Wilford Woodruff reported that Brigham Young thought the fullness of the priesthood was yet to be given: "If any in the Church had the fullness of the Melchisedec Priesthood, he [Brigham Young] did not know it." Clearly, though, Smith had at least discussed this concept with Young, who added, "For any person to have the fullness of that priesthood, he must be a king and a priest. . . . A person may be anointed king and priest long before he receives his kingdom."[18]

Other relevant facets of Mormon thinking had also matured by the time Brigham Young made this statement, notably a refinement in the LDS view of "eternal life." Prior to receiving the "three degrees of glory" vision in February 1832 (now D&C 76), Mormons, including Joseph Smith, understood "eternal life" in the same sense as other Protestants: an undifferentiated heaven as the only alternative to an undifferentiated hell. Even after 1832 and possibly as late as 1843, Smith apparently still conceived "eternal life" as dwelling in the presence of Elohim forever. It was not until May 1843 that Smith taught that the celestial kingdom contained gradations, with the highest gradation reserved solely for men and women who had entered into the new and everlasting covenant of marriage (see D&C 131:1-4). In July 1843, Smith dictated another revelation (now D&C 132) which defined those achieving "exaltation" in the highest degree of the celestial kingdom as "gods."

The importance of this teaching is seen in another Smith sermon given shortly thereafter on 27 August 1843. Significantly, these comments occurred in a discussion of three orders of priesthood: the Levitical, the patriarchal (or Abrahamic), and the fullness of the priesthood of Melchizedek which included "kingly powers" of "anointing & sealing—called elected and made sure."[19] Said Smith: "No man can attain to the Joint heirship with Jesus Christ with out being administered to by one having the same power & Authority of Melchisedec." This authority and power came not from "a Prophet nor apostle nor Patriarch only but of [a] King & Priest [of Jesus Christ]."[20]

In this same 27 August 1843 sermon Smith said that "Abraham[']s Patriarchal power" was the "greatest yet experienced in this church," implying that the fullness of the Melchizedek priesthood had not yet been introduced. His choice of words is particularly revealing considering the fact that by this date ten men had received the initiatory washings and anointings, as well as the Aaronic and Melchizedek portions of the endowments of the "Patriarchal Priesthood" on 2 May 1842. Many of these had also received the ordinance of celestial marriage for time and eternity with their wives. When Smith said late in August that the Patriarchal priesthood was the "greatest yet experienced in this church," he was well aware that the fullness of the Melchizedek priesthood was yet to be conferred through a higher ordinance.

In a sense the institution of this "higher ordinance" was the logical next step. The previous twelve years of pronouncements, sealings, and anointings "unto eternal life" guaranteed a status that, according to Smith's 1843 teachings, was subservient to that of the gods. From the perspective of these teachings, even the Nauvoo endowment administered to members of the "Holy Order" simply provided that the men who received it would live in the celestial kingdom as angels and servants. Until 1843, women had been excluded from these ordinances, possibly because of Joseph Smith's personal reluctance, Emma Smith's rejection of polygamy, John C. Bennett's lurid expose of polygamy, and/or the disaffection and subsequent reconciliation of Orson and Sarah Pratt over polygamy. However, Doctrine and Covenants 131 and 132 indicated that this exclusion deprived the men (who had received the previous ordinances) of the highest kingdom of glory—godhood. The higher ordinance was necessary to confirm the revealed promises of "kingly powers" (i.e., godhood) received in the endowment's initiatory ordinances. Godhood was therefore the meaning of this higher ordinance, or second anointing. The previously revealed promises in Doctrine and Covenants 132:19–26 implicitly referred not to those who had been sealed and ordained "kings and priests," "queens and priestesses" to God, not to those who had been sealed in celestial marriage. Such individuals, having received the "second anointing," would "be gods, because they have all power, and the angels are subject to them."

This special priesthood ordinance was first administered on 28 September 1843 to Joseph and Emma Smith. According to

Smith's personal journal: "Beurach Ale [Joseph Smith] was by common consent and unanimous voice chosen President of the quorum [of the anointed] and [was] anointed and ord[ained] to the highest and holiest order of the priesthood [as a king and a priest] (and companion [as a queen and a priestess])."[21] His "companion" was his wife, Emma, to whom he had been sealed for time and eternity four months earlier on 28 May. Wilford Woodruff's record of this event, found in his 1858 Historian's Private Office Journal, is equally explicit: "Then by common consent Joseph Smith the Prophet Received his second Anointing of the Highest & Holiest order."[22]

During the next five months this higher priesthood ordinance of the second anointing was conferred upon at least twenty men and the wives of sixteen of these men. Fullness of priesthood blessings during Joseph Smith's lifetime were reserved primarily for church leaders. An apparent reason for Smith's concern to complete the Nauvoo temple and administer the fullness of the priesthood to the twelve apostles was that these leaders were required to "round up their shoulders and bear it [the Mormon kingdom] off," for "the Kingdom will be established, and I do not care what shall become of me." As George Q. Cannon noted in 1869, "It was by the virtue of this authority [i.e., "endowment" and "holy anointing"], on the death of Joseph Smith, that President [Brigham] Young, as President of the quorum of the Twelve, presided over the Church."[23]

In an important discourse on priesthood on 10 March 1844, Joseph Smith was recorded as saying: "the spirit power & calling of Elijah is that ye have power to hold the keys of the revelations ordi-[n]ances, oricles powers & endowments of the fulness of the Melchizedek Priesthood & of the Kingdom of God on the Earth & to receive, obtain & perform all the ordinances belonging to the Kingdom of God even unto the sealing of the hearts of the hearts [sic] fathers unto the children & the hearts of the children unto the fathers even those who are in heaven."[24]

The fullness of this sealing power of Elijah, derived from the New Testament sealing authority of Jesus, completed the basic form of the priesthood endowment as the promise of ultimate exaltation while still in mortality. The constant reshuffling and recombining of theological and scriptural images during these early years could easily be termed "the fullness that was never full." At each step of the way, Smith proclaimed he had completed the organization of the church and had "passed through all the necessary ceremonies" or restored the "highest order of the Melchisedek Priesthood" only to introduce more revelations and theological innovations creating yet new layers of ritual, deposited on or integrated with the old.

Centrally embedded in the evolution of the anointing ritual in Mormon history was the theme of leadership. As the ritual evolved, lay members of the church advanced into the "inner circle," receiving ordinances and symbols formerly held only by Joseph Smith and his immediate circle, while Smith and his associates moved on to higher kingdoms, more sure promises, and more secret rituals. Although theological perceptions dealing with certain aspects of the Mormon concept of salvation as found in the endowment ritual — and, more particularly, the second anointing — underwent further modification, change in the fundamental framework of ritual and theology was frozen by Smith's death in June 1844.

— NOTES —

1. Joseph Smith, Jr., et al., *History of the Church of Jesus Christ of Latter-day Saints*, ed. B. H. Roberts, 7 vols. (Salt Lake City: Deseret Book Co., 1973), 1:175–76; hereafter HC.

2. David Whitmer, *An Address to All Believers in Christ* (Richmond, MO: n.p., 1887), 64, 35; see also 32, 49, 62, 63, 65.

3. "Far West Record," archives, Church of Jesus Christ of Latter-day Saints, Salt Lake City, Utah, hereafter church archives; see also Donald Q. Cannon and Lyndon W. Cook, eds., *Far West Record, Minutes of The Church of Jesus Christ of Latter-day Saints* (Salt Lake City: Deseret Book, 1982), 20–21.

4. This story seems to have been patterned after the account of Elijah the Tishbite "sealing" the heavens by drought in 1 Kings 17; also compare the Nephi-Elijah connection in He. 5:30 and 1 Kings 19:11–12.

5. Zebedee Coltrin Diary, 15 Nov. 1831, church archives.

6. In some ways, this ordinance parallels that revealed in D&C 60:15 and 84:92 wherein priesthood bearers are authorized to "seal up" wicked persons to a damning judgment with a washing-of-the-feet and shaking-off-the-dust ceremony. This "ordinance of damnation" could also be performed with reference to a group of people at once.

7. HC 1:322–23.

8. Ibid., 323.

9. Ibid., 2:379–82.

10. Ibid., 391–92.

11. Ibid., 410–28.

12. Ibid., 429–30.

13. Ibid., 430–33.

14. Andrew F. Ehat and Lyndon W. Cook, comps. and eds., *The Words of Joseph Smith: The Contemporary Accounts of the Nauvoo Discourses of the Prophet Joseph Smith* (Provo, UT: BYU Religious Studies Center, 1980), 4; see also HC 3:379–81.

15. For discussions of this group and the Nauvoo temple endowment, see D. Michael Quinn, "Latter-day Saints Prayer Circles," *Brigham Young University Studies* 19 (Fall 1978): 84–96; Andrew F. Ehat, "Joseph Smith's Introduction of Temple Ordinances and the 1844 Mormon Succession Question," M.A. thesis, Brigham Young University, 1982, 24–188; and my "The Development of the Mormon Temple Endowment Ceremony," *Dialogue: A Journal of Mormon Thought* 20 (Winter 1987): 36–49.

16. HC 5:1–2.

17. Ibid., 139–40.

18. Ibid., 527.

19. Ehat and Cook, 244. Smith apparently believed that the patriarchal priesthood—which related to the "lower" ordinances of the temple endowment—"comprehended" the Levitical priesthood but was different from the fullness of the Melchizedek priesthood.

20. Ibid., 245.

21. Joseph Smith Journal, 28 Sept. 1843, church archives, in Scott H. Faulring, ed., *An American Prophet's Record: The Diaries and Journals of Joseph Smith* (Salt Lake City: Signature Books and Smith Research Associates, 1987), 416; cf. HC 6:39.

22. Wilford Woodruff, Historian's Private Office Journal, 1858, church archives.

23. *Journal of Discourses*, 26 vols. (Liverpool: LDS Book Depot, 1855–86), 13:49.

24. Ehat and Cook, 329.

15.
Eternal Progression and the Second Death in the Theology of Brigham Young

Boyd Kirkland

ACCORDING TO CONTEMPORARY MORMON THEOLOGY, GODS, AN-gels, mortals, and even devils are members of the same eternal family but at different stages of development. The difference among them is determined by their obedience to eternal laws. This concept of "eternal progression" undergirds the church's notion of preexistence, mortality, and the afterlife. It renders Mormon theology radically different from traditional Judeo-Christian theology, which views God as the only self-existing reality and considers angels, mortals, and devils as creatures totally dependant—or contingent—upon God for their existence.

Despite its importance to Mormon theology, eternal progression has been variously interpreted since the church's beginnings. For example, some of the ideas of Brigham Young, second president of the LDS church, are relatively unknown to church members today and are even considered heretical by some twentieth-century Mormon leaders. Likewise, Young's beliefs about the "second death," which he advocated as the logical opposite to eternal progression, seem to have died with him. Where eternal progression concerns the origin and future of gods, eternal retrogression, or the second death, concerns the origin and future of devils. Young usually discussed these two concepts together, contrasting them with each other to illustrate more clearly the nature of each. In what follows I will explore Brigham Young's teachings on these subjects, particularly the second death.

The earliest writings of church founder Joseph Smith, from whom Brigham Young took his lead in theological speculation, reflect an absolutist trinitarian theology with a primitivist Protestant influence. God is creator—eternal and self-existent; he spoke the cosmos into existence for man, his special creation made in his image. Man is creature, wholly dependant upon God for his existence; and because of the Fall, he is essentially depraved and unworthy of God's presence. Therefore, he must prove himself, by accepting the "infinite and eternal" atonement made for his sins by God as Christ and by obeying God's commandments. Satan and his followers are fallen angels, who tempt man to disobey God and with whom God shall condemn the unrighteous to Hell. God will reward the righteous by returning them to his presence in heaven, where they will sing ceaseless praises to him forever. Man's banishment from God's presence in this world is "spiritual death." Following final judgment, those who do not prove worthy of salvation will be banished from God's presence a second time with Satan and his angels, suffering the "second death" or second separation from God.[1]

Later Joseph Smith revised his thinking about the nature of God and man. He no longer considered God to be totally and uniquely uncontingent but began to teach that man and the elements of the universe are also self-existing and eternal (D&C 93:33). Further, he portrayed God as a temporal being occupying space and existing in time (D&C 130:4–9, 22; Abr. 3:3, 9, 18; 5:13). Sometime in his past, God was as man now is, but as he learned obedience to eternal laws, he progressed to godhood. Man's spirit, coequal with and of the same nature as God, is capable of this same progression (Abr. 3:18; D&C 93:23, 29).[2] The ideas that God progressed to godhood and that men and women could become gods themselves logically implied the existence of a plurality of gods. Indeed, Smith taught that God himself has a father, or god, to whom he is accountable. Just how far back Smith believed this paternal line of gods extended is unclear. At times, he hinted at the existence of an ultimate god to whom all other gods are answerable and who directs the lesser gods in their creation efforts (D&C 121:32).

Since Smith thought that all matter was uncreated and eternal, he reasoned that God creates by organizing these preexisting materials (Abr. 3:24; 4:1). But that which can be organized can be disorganized; that which has a beginning can have an ending. Thus Smith believed that the spirit of man, to be truly eternal, never had a beginning. God's creative work is to provide the opportunity and environment for man to progress from one stage of existence to another. Smith taught that life came to this earth through procreation, not special creation.[3] His doctrine of celestial marriage, by which men and women are sealed together for eternity, promised that the seed of those so married would continue forever. The parents could thus create and populate future worlds, presiding over them as gods (D&C 131:1–4; 132:19–20, 30, 63).

Satan and his followers are also self-existent spirits, who, prior to the creation of the world, rebelled against God. Cast out of God's presence, they forever forfeited their right to progress into mortality with the more valiant spirits. Those spirits who entered mortality are being tested to determine their worthiness to progress further along the road to godhood. The vast majority will receive some form of redemption and be resurrected to one of three "kingdoms of glory." Only the "sons of perdition," who commit the "unpardonable sin" against the Holy Ghost, will be resurrected to a kingdom of no glory, where they will suffer the "second death" of eternal banishment from God into outer darkness along with Satan and his followers (D&C 76:19–113; 88:3–39). Smith reported that this torment was too terrible to describe fully (D&C 76:43–48) and later added that the sons of perdition would never be redeemed: "There also have been remarks made concerning all men being redeemed from hell, but those who sin against the Holy Ghost cannot be forgiven in this world or in the world to come. But I say that those who commit the unpardonable sin are doomed to *Gnolaum*, and must dwell in hell, worlds without end; they shall die the second death."[4]

Joseph Smith's early, more absolutist teachings and his later, more progressive doctrines exist side-by-side in Mormon canon. However, his most innovative views were only taught publicly just before his death in 1844 and have never been canonized. The differences between these two approaches have proven troublesome to many Mormon theologians who have long tried to reconcile these seemingly irreconcilable views. They have sometimes offered diluted interpretations of Smith's more controversial statements or

have challenged the historical accuracy of the statements themselves. The same is true of some Mormon writers' attempts to deal
with the equally radical theology of Brigham Young.

For their part, neither Young nor Smith paid much attention
to this apparent dichotomy. Rather than try to reconcile the two
teachings, they simply abandoned earlier Mormon theology in favor
of later doctrines. Although both men claimed that there were no
differences between the teachings of ancient apostles and prophets
and those of the modern restorers of God's truth,[5] they did not feel
the need to justify their new doctrines by reconciling them with
scripture. When they did occasionally use scripture, however, they
focused on present needs with little regard to original context and
meaning. In fact Young maintained that the scriptures were written
according to our readiness to receive truth. If Young's views differed
from the scriptures, it was only because he was better prepared to
receive the truth than the ancient authors. Young thus continued to
promote and elaborate on Smith's later theology, sometimes even
revising Smith's doctrines to better suit his own unfolding views.

For example, Smith did not seem to believe that the spirit of
man had a beginning. But Young taught that the spirit was literally
begotten by heavenly parents.[6] Young expanded Smith's teaching
that all life began on this earth through procreation, explaining that
God had transplanted the Earth's plant and animal life from another world. Similarly, Young believed that God and one of his plural wives voluntarily descended from heaven to become Adam and
Eve, the parents of the human race. God's father presided in his
place while he enacted the role of Adam.[7]

Although consistent with Smith's concept of a plurality of
gods, Young's teachings rejected the possibility of an ultimate god to
whom all other gods are accountable. He believed in an endless
chain of gods extending back into the eternities with no beginning
and which would continue into the future with no end.[8] This infinite
line of gods formed a patriarchal hierarchy, along which the "presiding god" at any one point would be the one who presided over those
below him. According to Young, God's role as Adam was a one-time
"calling"; his next responsibility would be to preside as "grandfather" over his own posterity, who would, if they proved worthy, act
as Adams and Eves of their own worlds.[9]

Like Smith, Young believed that space, time, and matter

exist eternally. He evidently did not envision the universe as a closed system but as an infinite system with no boundaries. An infinite supply of matter must exist, which an infinite line of future gods use to organize worlds without number for their spirit children who are born in infinite numbers.[10] Young also believed that the entire universe either progresses or retrogresses: "All organized existence is in progress, either to an endless advancement in eternal perfections, or back to dissolution."[11]

Just as he saw no limits to the physical universe, Young saw no limits to the possible progression of mortals and gods. Although men and women would be assigned to a kingdom in the next life according to their merits, they could still progress within their assigned kingdom and eventually advance to higher kingdoms.[12] This process of progression would never cease, even for the gods who would eternally acquire more dominion, knowledge, and power. Young reasoned that limiting the amount of knowledge one could attain was equivalent to limiting the universe itself.[13] He taught that only the devils and the sons of perdition themselves, who had consciously decided to rebel against God, would ever cease to learn and progress.[14]

Although Smith declined to reveal the full extent of the terrible sufferings of the sons of perdition, Young was more willing to speculate on the second death: "When the elements in an organized form do not fill the end of their creation, they are thrown back again . . . to be ground up, and made over again. . . . And if he [Jesus] ever makes 'a *full end* of the wicked,' what else can he do than entirely disorganize them and reduce them to their native element?"[15] "The first death," he explained, "is the separation of the spirit from the body; the second death is . . . the dissolution of the organized particles which compose the spirit, and their return to their native element."[16] The second death, he warned, is "the death that never dies."[17] "To refuse life and choose death," he stressed, "is to *refuse* an eternal existence in an organized capacity, and be contented to become decomposed, and return again to native element. . . . The one leads to endless increase and progression, the other to the destruction of the organized being, ending in its entire decomposition into the particles that compose the native elements."[18]

Young did not believe that man has a conscious, self-existing identity separate from his spirit. Rather, he thought that spirits were made of uncreated, raw intelligence, and predicted that devils and sons of perdition will eventually cease to exist as conscious entities: "If you do not obey [the Lord's] voice, it will prove that you are not worthy of intelligence, any more than the clay upon the potter's wheel: consequently, the intelligence that you are endowed with will be taken from you, and you will have to go into the mill and be ground over again."[19] A person who returns to this state will cease to exist. But because of the eternal nature of matter, this return to native element does not necessarily mean complete annihilation: "When people take the downward road, one that is calculated to destroy them, they will actually in every sense of the word be destroyed. Will they be what is termed annihilated? No, there is no such thing as annihilation, for you cannot destroy the elements of which things are made."[20]

Young implied, like Smith, that this rebellion can occur at any stage of one's progression: during the preexistence, during mortality, or even following the resurrection. "Suppose," Young hypothesized, "that our Father in heaven, our elder brother, the risen Redeemer, ... or any of the Gods of eternity should [abuse their power] ... to torment the people of the earth, exercise sovereignty over them, and make them miserable at their pleasure; they would cease to be Gods; and as fast as they adopted and acted upon such principles, they would become devils, and be thrust down in the twinkling of an eye; the extension of their kingdom would cease, and their God-head come to an end."[21]

Young also speculated that Satan, before rebelling against God, was probably a resurrected son of perdition from a previous world. He believed that prior to their eternal dissolution, the resurrected sons of perdition from this earth would be used by the Lord as devils for future worlds: "We expect all who are faithful to take the place of Adams in the worlds to be created; then if there were no apostates, what would we do for Devils? As we have to get our devils from this earth, for the worlds that are to be created."[22] "Men in the flesh are clothed with the Priesthood and its blessings, the apostatizing from which and turning away from the Lord prepares them to become sons of perdition," he added, hinting at the future role of sons of perdition as devils. "There was a Devil in heaven, and he strove to possess the birthright of the Savior. He was a liar from the beginning, and loves those who live and make lies, as do his imps and followers here on earth. How many devils there are in heaven, or where it is, is not for me to say."[23]

The Mormon temple endowment scenario, which Young codified, also suggests that Young believed Satan once possessed a physical body. The endowment depicts Satan as Adam's peer who lived with him on a previous world which provided the pattern for the creation of this earth. The fact that Young believed that Adam had been resurrected prior to coming to this earth implies that Satan also was resurrected. Could Young have interpreted the serpent's curse in the Garden of Eden — the loss of its arms and legs, being forced to crawl upon its belly in the dust — as a metaphor for Satan's loss of a physical body as part of this process of decomposition? In the endowment, Satan does lose his apron, a symbol of his "power and priesthoods," after being cursed in the Garden of Eden. Although speculation, Young did teach that part of Satan's curse was that he would not possess a physical body, that he would eventually decompose even spiritually, return to the eternal spirit element from which he was created, and become as if he did not exist.

While Joseph Smith offered no hope of redemption for the sons of perdition, Young taught that the elemental matter of such disorganized individuals might be reconstituted: "The rebellious will be thrown back into their native element, there to remain myriads of years before their dust will again be revived, before they will be re-organized."[24] "Worked over again," they will "sooner or later" be "prepared to enjoy some sort of kingdom." Although it is unclear if Young believed such "reorganized" individuals will have the same intelligence and identity as they did previously, this seems unlikely in light of his teachings that the sons of perdition would cease to exist.[25] Thus his concept holds little comfort for those who fear that the wicked would have a "second chance."

Just as Joseph Smith's later teachings troubled some followers, Young's additional speculations have for the most part been coolly received. Apostle Orson Pratt publicly and privately opposed many of Young's teachings, specifically disagreeing that the second death means a dissolution of the body and spirit: "[The] second death [is] not a dissolution of body and spirit like that of the first death, but a banishment from the presence of God, and from the glory of his power."[26] "Suppose I ask the learned when was the beginning of eternity?" Young countered. "Can they think of it? No!

And I should very much doubt some of the sayings of one of the best philosophers and writers of the age, that we call brother [i.e., Pratt], with regard to the character of the Lord God whom we serve. I very much doubt whether it has ever entered into his heart to compre-hend eternity."[27]

Other church authorities defended Young's teachings, how-ever, including Heber C. Kimball,[28] Erastus Snow,[29] Daniel H. Wells,[30] and Wilford Woodruff.[31] But after Young's death in 1877, many of his doctrines were apologized for, reinterpreted, repudi-ated, or simply denied to have ever been taught. Much of this took place at the turn of the century, when the church was trying to improve its public image and refining its diverse doctrinal heritage into a more concise, harmonious theology. The only view of the second death the church retained was the Book of Mormon's tradi-tionalist description of spiritual separation from God. Church leader (and later president) Joseph F. Smith typified this position in 1895. "The first death which came into the world is also the last death which shall be pronounced upon the sons of perdition," he said. "What is it? Banishment from the presence of God. . . . This is what I understand spiritual death is. I do not understand it to be the sepa-ration of the body and spirit again. I do not understand it to be the dissolution of the spirit into its native element. I understand the second death to be the same as the first death." Resurrected men and women "are immortal beings," he continued, "and they are destined, if they commit the unpardonable sin, to be banished from the pres-ence of God, and endure the punishment of the devil and his angels throughout all eternity. I think that the wicked would prefer annihi-lation to the sufferings of such punishment—an end to being. This view cannot be reconciled to the word of God."[32] Joseph F. Smith rejected Young's second death doctrine because, in his mind, it con-tradicted the scriptural description of the second death as being a separation from God, it conflicted with the perception of a bodily resurrection as a final, immutable condition, and it somehow vio-lated the demands of justice which require prolonged, or even eter-nal, suffering and punishment for the wicked.

These arguments seem to stem back to the more conserva-tive, Protestant-influenced theology canonized in Joseph Smith's earlier days. But Smith himself departed radically form his own teachings, giving precedent for Young's additional innovations. Still,

I doubt that Smith would have accepted Young's second death doctrine. His reasons would not necessarily be those later elucidated by Joseph F. Smith; instead, he would probably have felt that it contradicted his view of the unbegotten, eternal nature of the spirit, which he believed coexists eternally with God. Like Joseph Smith, Young did not feel the need to justify his doctrines scripturally. Once he died, however, many of his ideas failed to find a strong vocal advocate among the leaders of the church, including his second death doctrine.

Personally, I find the internal logic and liberal nature of many of Young's ideas of eternal progression appealing. Although they are not always totally harmonious with Joseph Smith's views, they at least continue the inventive doctrinal trend Smith began in Nauvoo. But ultimately both men's views were influenced and limited by nineteenth-century scientific theories as well as by scriptural traditions grounded in mythology centuries old. Still, their willingness to strike out into unchartered theological waters gives Mormons today intriguing and unique responses to the ageless quest for life's meaning. Sailing upon the open seas of theological speculation has some risks, but no ship ever discovered new ports while anchored in the harbor.

– NOTES –

1. See 1 Ne. 11:16–18, 21; 2 Ne. 2:17–18, 22; 9:7, 8, 10–12, 20–23; Jac. 4:9; Mos. 2:21, 23, 25, 28, 38–39, 41; 3:5, 11, 15–21, 25–27; 4:2, 5, 9, 11; 5:2, 15; 7:27; 13:28; 15:1–5; 16:3–5; Al. 12:16–18, 22, 24, 32; 22:10; 26:35; 34:9–16; 32–35; 41:4; 42:4, 9–10, 13–16; He. 14:16–18; 3 Ne. 11:14; Morm. 7:7; 9:17, 19; Eth. 3:4; Moro. 7:22; 8:18; D&C 19:16–19; 20:12, 17, 28; 29:31–33; 36–44; 38:1–3; 45:1; 61:1; 76:4, 25–29; 88:41; 93:10; Moses 1:3, 6, 33, 35, 37, 38; 2:1, 5–7, 11, 16, 30; 3:6, 7,; 4:1, 25; 6:48–49, 54–55; 7:29; but compare 1 Ne. 14:3 and Al. 42:9, 16 with 2 Ne. 1:17, 22 and Al. 36:15, where the possibility of annihilation seems somewhat ambiguous.

2. See Stan Larson, "The King Follett Discourse: A Newly Amalgamated Text," *Brigham Young University Studies* 18 (Winter 1978), 2:198–225. For Brigham Young's views on God's being subject to law, see Brigham Young, et. al, *Journal of Discourses*, 26 vols. (Liverpool: Latter-day Saints' Book Depot, 1855–86), 14:71–72 (hereafter JD, followed by volume and page numbers).

3. See, for example, Andrew F. Ehat and Lyndon W. Cook, *The*

Words of Joseph Smith (Provo, UT: Religious Studies Center, Brigham Young University, 1980), 380.

4. In Larson, 207–208.

5. JD 5:329.

6. In supervising some of Joseph Smith's public sermons for publication, Brigham Young changed Smith's statements that the *spirit* of man has no beginning and is coequal with God to refer instead to the *intelligence* of man's spirit as having no beginning, thus changing Smith's original meaning. See Van Hale, "The Origin of the Human Spirit in Early Mormon Thought," in this compilation.

7. See Brigham Young, unpublished sermons, 8 Oct. 1854 and 25 Aug. 1867, historical department, Church of Jesus Christ of Latter-day Saints, Salt Lake City (hereafter church archives); JD 1:50; 3:318; 7:285; 9:148.

8. Brigham Young, unpublished sermons, 8 Oct. 1854 and 10 Aug. 1862, church archives; JD 9:243.

9. See Scott G. Kenney, ed., *Wilford Woodruff's Journal*, 9 vols. (Midvale, UT: Signature Books, 1983–85), 4:317; JD 4:271; 8:61, 208; 12:97; Samuel W. Richards Journal, 11 March 1856, church archives. Technically, Young implied that God could continue to create and populate worlds eternally, continually reenacting the Adam role as often as he desired, if he had a sufficient number of wives and posterity.

10. Brigham Young, unpublished sermons, 8 Oct. 1854 and 10 Aug. 1862; JD 1:275–76; 9:243.

11. JD 1:349. Young wanted to build the Salt Lake Temple from adobe rather than granite. He believed that adobe would last longer because it was becoming rock but granite had already reached the extent of its progression and would soon begin to deteriorate (JD 1:218–20). Young taught that the entire earth would continue to progress until it would ultimately be redeemed and be made into a celestial world, returning to its place of origin near the throne of God (unpublished sermon, 8 Oct. 1854; JD 17:144).

12. Kenney, 4:333–34. Joseph Smith's older brother Hyrum publicly taught during Smith's lifetime that "Those of the Terrestrial Glory either advance to the Celestial or recede to the Telestial" (Franklin D. Richards, "Scriptural Items," 1 Aug. 1843, church archives). See also Gary James Bergera, "Grey Matters: Is There Progression Among the Eternal Kingdoms?" *Dialogue: A Journal of Mormon Thought* 15 (Spring 1982), 1:181–83.

13. JD 8:17; Kenney, 4:288; 5:439; *Deseret News* 22:308–309. Contrast Young's views here with those of twentieth-century apostle Bruce R. McConkie, "Eternal Progression," *Mormon Doctrine* (Salt Lake City: Bookcraft,

1966), 239; and "The Seven Deadly Heresies," *1980 Devotional Speeches of the Year* (Provo, UT: BYU Press, 1981).

14. See JD 3:203.

15. JD 1:275.

16. Ibid., 9:149.

17. Ibid., 8:28.

18. Ibid., 1:349, 352.

19. Ibid., 5:341; see also 4:31–32; 5:53–54; 6:333, 347; 7:57, 193, 203, 287.

20. Ibid., 2:302; see also 1:116–18.

21. Ibid., 1:116–17.

22. Historian's Office Journal, Aug. 1859, church archives; see also JD 4:363–64, 372; 8:179, 204, 279.

23. JD 8:279–80.

24. Ibid., 1:118.

25. Ibid., 5:53–54; 5:124; see also 8:197.

26. Ibid., 1:329–30; see also 7:255, 258.

27. Ibid., 1:352; see also 1:276. For others of Pratt's and Young's doctrinal disagreements, see Gary James Bergera, "The Orson Pratt-Brigham Young Controversies: Conflict Within the Quorums, 1853 to 1868," *Dialogue: A Journal of Mormon Thought* 13 (Summer 1980), 2:7–49.

28. JD 2:151–52; 4:363–64; 5:95, 249, 271, 273–74; 6:67; 8:240; 9:372.

29. Ibid., 7:352–54, 358–59; 8:216; 13:9.

30. Ibid., 9:43–44, 65, 83, 358; 12:132, 135.

31. Ibid., 9:163.

32. *Improvement Era* 19, 5:386–91.

Epilogue: "Continuing Revelation and Mormon Doctrine"

Stephen L Richards

I INTERPRET THE GOSPEL IN TERMS OF LIFE. IT WAS BROUGHT TO humanity; it is our duty to bring humanity to the gospel. Election not compulsion is the genius of Christian philosophy. Ridicule and ostracism often amount to compulsion. I deplore their existence. I fear dogmatism. It is a tyrant guilty of more havoc to humankind than the despot ruling over many kingdoms. . . .

The church believes in new and continuous revelation and ever holds itself in readiness to receive messages from the Lord. To that end the people sustain the president in particular and others of the General Authorities as the media through which God's word may be delivered. A revelation to our living president would be as readily accepted and become as much a part of our scripture as the revelations given to the Prophet Joseph [Smith].

In the absence of direct communication from heaven, however, the church and its people must be guided by the revelations already given and the wisdom and inspiration of its leadership. I have great confidence in the wisdom of the presiding authorities in all departments of church service, first, because they hold the holy priesthood and second, because I know them to be good men. . . .

In matters of church government and discipline, the judgment of presiding officers is mandatory and controlling. In matters of individual guidance to members, their counsel is directory and persuasive only. In the interpretation of scripture and doctrine, they are dependent on their knowledge and experience and inspiration.

I make this frank avowal of my own personal understanding of these fundamental principles as a premise to certain observations and conclusions I desire to present. The views I give I trust sincerely will not be repugnant to those held by my brethren.

First, I hold that it is entirely compatible with the genius of the church to change its procedure, forms, and interpretations as changes in thought, education, and environment of people from time to time seem to warrant, provided, of course, that no violence is done to the elemental concepts of truth which lie at the basis of our work. I would not discard a practice merely because it is old. Indeed, I believe that one of the tests of worth is the test of time. But, on the other hand, I would not hang on to a practice or conception after it has outlived its usefulness in a new and ever-changing and better-informed world.

Old conceptions and traditional interpretations must be influenced by newly discovered evidence. Not that ultimate fact and law change, but our understanding varies with our education and experience. One man sees the meaning of a scripture so clearly and definitely that he exclaims with contemptible deprecation of a contender's view, "Why it's as plain as the nose on your face," and the other replies, "It is silly and foolish." Both are sincere. Who is right? What position does the church take? Generally, I think, the church takes no official position and ought not to in the large majority of mooted questions. Men are permitted to hold individual views and express them with freedom so long as they are not seditious to the basic doctrines, practices, and establishments of the church. When men lose their regard for the church, of course, they are no longer entitled to place and influence in it.

I believe it appropriate to reannounce what I hope is a generally accepted proposition in our church that no man's standing is affected by the views which he may honestly hold with reference to the beginning of man's life on the earth and organization of the universe or the processes employed in the working of the miracles of the Bible. Personally I find more peace of mind and comfort in what may seem a rather lazy disposition to attempt no explanation of these seemingly inexplicable matters. But if anyone holds views and gets satisfaction from them, I say let him have them, and for one I won't abuse him for them. . . .

Another aspect of the changing process that must necessarily go forward in a live, vital institution such as the church is relates to the modification of forms and procedure. We do not have a great body of set forms and rituals, I am glad to say. The very elasticity of prayers, ceremonies, and procedure is additional evidence to me of the adaptability of our religion to human needs and therefore of its divinity. Some important changes have been made in recent years. In some instances they have considerably disturbed some members of the church. I am sure that the concern and alarm so created have been unwarranted. The critics have failed to recall that the items which have been modified were originally interpreted and adapted by good men occupying the same ecclesiastical positions and endowed with the same power as the good men now occupying these positions. Personally, I highly approve of the changes that have been made, and I hope and believe that the presiding authority will be led to make other changes along various lines that will advance the cause we represent. I am not afraid of change: it is the mother of growth. . . .

Dogmatism and bigotry have been the deadliest enemies of true religion in the long past. They have made it forbidding, shut it up in cold grey walls of monastery and nunnery out of the sunlight and fragrance of the growing world. They have garbed it in black and then in white, when in truth it is neither black nor white any more than life is black or white, for religion is life abundant, glowing life, with all its shades, colors, and hues, as the children of men reflect in the patterns of their lives the radiance of the Holy Spirit in varying degrees.

CONTRIBUTORS

Thomas G. Alexander is a professor of American history at Brigham Young University.

Peter C. Appleby is a professor of philosophy at the University of Utah.

George Boyd, retired, taught seminary and institute of religion classes for the educational system of the Church of Jesus Christ of Latter-day Saints.

David John Buerger is an executive editor of *InfoWorld* newsweekly.

Van Hale is the publisher of the *Mormon Miscellaneous* reprint and pamphlet series.

Boyd Kirkland is a producer and artist for the animation industry in Los Angeles.

Blake Oslter is an attorney in Salt Lake City.

Stephen L Richards was a General Authority of the Church of Jesus Christ of Latter-day Saints from 1917 until his death in 1959.

Kent E. Robson is a professor of philosophy at Utah State University.

Thaddeus E. Shoemaker is a professor of government at California State University, Sacramento.

Vern Swanson is the director of the Springville, Utah, Art Museum.

Dan Vogel is the author of *Indian Origins and the Book of Mormon* and *Religious Seekers and the Advent of Mormonism*.

Linda P. Wilcox, a graduate of Stanford University and the University of Utah, is employed by Salt Lake County.